Computer Programming Essentials

A Comprehensive and Easy Handbook for Beginners

Jerry P. G. Bill

TABLE OF CONTENTS

Computer Programming Essentials

Computer Programming Essentials

Computer Programming Essentials

Computer Programming Essentials

Computer Programming Essentials

Computer Programming Essentials

Computer Programming Essentials

Computer Programming Essentials

K
L
M
N
O
P
Q
R
S
T
U
V
W
X
Y
Z

Computer Programming Essentials

Introduction to Programming

What is Programming?

Programming is the process of designing, writing, testing, and maintaining the instructions, called code, that computers follow to perform specific tasks. These instructions are written in programming languages that computers can understand and execute. Programming bridges the gap between human ideas and the mechanical functionality of computers, enabling machines to automate tasks, analyze data, solve problems, and create interactive experiences.

At its core, programming involves three primary components:

1. **Logic:** Designing algorithms and processes to solve problems or achieve desired outcomes.
2. **Syntax:** Using the rules of a programming language to express logic in a format the computer can interpret.
3. **Execution:** Running the written code on a machine to perform the intended operation.

Programming is fundamental in various fields, including web development, artificial intelligence, robotics, scientific research, mobile app development, and more.

History of Programming Languages

The history of programming languages reflects the evolution of technology and human ingenuity. Here are key milestones:

1. **Early Foundations (1940s-1950s):**

- ○ Programming began with machine code, a low-level language consisting of binary digits (0s and 1s) directly understood by hardware.
- ○ **Assembly Language** was introduced as a symbolic representation of machine code, simplifying the process of writing instructions.
- ○ The first high-level programming language, **FORTRAN (FORmula TRANslation)**, was developed in the 1950s for scientific and engineering calculations.

2. **Expansion and Specialization (1960s-1970s):**

- ○ The 1960s saw the creation of languages like **COBOL** for business applications and **ALGOL**, which influenced many future programming languages.

- In 1970, **Pascal** emerged as a teaching language, promoting structured programming concepts.
- The development of **C** in the early 1970s revolutionized programming with its balance of efficiency and flexibility, becoming the basis for many modern languages.

3. **The Object-Oriented Era (1980s):**

- **Smalltalk** introduced the concept of Object-Oriented Programming (OOP), emphasizing modularity and reuse.
- **C++**, an extension of C, incorporated OOP features and became widely adopted for software development.

4. **The Internet Age (1990s):**

- The rise of the internet drove the development of web-oriented languages like **HTML**, **JavaScript**, and **PHP**.

- ○ **Java**, introduced in 1995, became popular for its "write once, run anywhere" philosophy, making it ideal for cross-platform applications.
- ○ Scripting languages like **Python** gained traction due to their simplicity and readability.

5. **Modern Programming (2000s-Present):**

- ○ Languages like **Ruby**, **Swift**, **Kotlin**, and **Go** cater to specific modern needs, such as mobile development, simplicity, and scalability.
- ○ The emphasis on parallel computing, AI, and machine learning led to the popularity of frameworks and tools in languages like **Python** and **R**.
- ○ Functional programming gained renewed interest with languages like **Scala**, **Haskell**, and modern adaptations of existing languages.

Programming languages continue to evolve, adapting to technological advancements and addressing emerging challenges.

The Role of a Programmer

A programmer, also known as a software developer or coder, is a professional who designs, writes, tests, and maintains software applications. Their role extends beyond merely writing code; they are problem-solvers and innovators who enable technology to meet human needs.

Key responsibilities include:

1. **Analyzing Requirements:** Understanding the needs of users or clients to design appropriate software solutions.
2. **Developing Algorithms:** Crafting logical steps to solve problems effectively and efficiently.

3. **Writing Code:** Using programming languages to implement algorithms in a functional, maintainable format.
4. **Testing and Debugging:** Ensuring software performs as intended by identifying and fixing errors or inefficiencies.
5. **Collaborating with Teams:** Working with designers, project managers, and other developers to create cohesive and functional systems.
6. **Maintaining Software:** Updating applications to fix bugs, adapt to new requirements, or enhance performance.

Skills and Qualities of a Programmer:

- **Technical Expertise:** Proficiency in programming languages, frameworks, and tools.
- **Problem-Solving:** Analytical thinking to design efficient solutions.
- **Adaptability:** Learning new technologies and staying updated with industry trends.

- **Attention to Detail:** Ensuring precision in code to avoid errors.
- **Communication Skills:** Explaining technical concepts and collaborating effectively.

Programmers play a pivotal role in shaping modern society by creating technologies that drive innovation, efficiency, and connectivity. From developing critical software for industries to crafting entertainment experiences, their work impacts virtually every aspect of our lives.

Getting Started with Programming

Setting Up Your Development Environment

Before you can start programming, you need to set up a development environment—a combination of tools and software that allows you to write, test, and debug your code efficiently.

Steps to Set Up a Development Environment:

1. **Choose Your Programming Language:** Decide which programming language you want to learn or work with. Popular options for beginners include Python, JavaScript, and Java. Each language may have specific tools and setups.

2. **Install a Code Editor or IDE:** Select a code editor or Integrated Development Environment (IDE) based on your chosen language. Examples include:

   - **VS Code:** A lightweight yet powerful editor with extensive plugins for multiple languages.
   - **PyCharm:** Tailored for Python development.
   - **Eclipse/IntelliJ IDEA:** Commonly used for Java programming.
   - **Notepad++ or Sublime Text:** Simple editors for general use.

3. **Install the Compiler/Interpreter:** Depending on the language, you may

need to install software that translates your code into machine-readable instructions.

- ○ **Python:** Install the Python interpreter.
- ○ **C/C++:** Use compilers like GCC or Clang.
- ○ **Java:** Install the Java Development Kit (JDK).

4. **Set Up Version Control (Optional):** Version control tools like **Git** allow you to track changes in your code and collaborate with others. Install Git and create a GitHub account to manage your projects.

5. **Configure Environment Variables:** Some programming tools require setting environment variables (e.g., PATH) so your system can find necessary executables. Most installations provide instructions for this step.

6. **Install Additional Tools (If Needed):**
   Depending on your goals, you might need additional software, such as:

   ○ Database management systems (e.g., MySQL, PostgreSQL) for database development.
   ○ Web servers (e.g., Apache, Nginx) for web development.
   ○ Libraries and frameworks specific to your project, which can often be installed via package managers like pip (Python), npm (JavaScript), or Maven (Java).

Understanding Integrated Development Environments (IDEs)

An Integrated Development Environment (IDE) is a comprehensive tool that simplifies programming by combining a code editor, compiler or interpreter, debugger, and other features in a single interface.

Benefits of Using an IDE:

- **Efficiency:** Automates repetitive tasks, such as code compilation and execution.
- **Error Detection:** Highlights syntax errors and offers suggestions while you code.
- **Debugging Tools:** Helps identify and fix errors with built-in debugging capabilities.
- **Code Management:** Organizes files and folders for complex projects.
- **Autocomplete:** Provides intelligent suggestions for code completion.

Popular IDEs and Their Features:

1. **Visual Studio Code (VS Code):**

   - Lightweight and highly customizable through extensions.
   - Supports multiple languages and features built-in Git integration.

2. **PyCharm:**

○ Optimized for Python with powerful debugging and testing tools.

○ Includes features like code navigation and database tools.

3. **IntelliJ IDEA:**

○ Ideal for Java development, with strong refactoring tools and code analysis.

○ Provides built-in support for popular frameworks like Spring and Hibernate.

4. **Eclipse:**

○ Versatile IDE for Java, C++, and other languages.

○ Includes tools for modeling, debugging, and code generation.

5. **IDLE (Python):**

○ A simple IDE bundled with Python for beginners.

> ○ Suitable for small projects and
> learning the basics.

When to Use a Simple Editor vs. an IDE:

- **Simple Editors (e.g., Notepad++,
  Sublime Text):**
  Use for lightweight projects, scripting, or
  quick edits.
- **IDEs:**
  Use for larger, complex projects where
  features like debugging and version
  control are essential.

Writing Your First Program

Writing your first program is a significant step in
learning programming. Let's use Python, a
beginner-friendly language, to demonstrate the
process.

Steps to Write Your First Program:

1. **Open Your IDE or Code Editor:**
   Launch your preferred development environment. For Python, you can use IDLE or VS Code.

2. **Create a New File:**
   In your editor, create a new file and save it with an appropriate extension. For Python, use .py (e.g., first_program.py).

Write Your Code:
Type the following code, which outputs a simple message to the screen:

```
print("Hello, World!")
```

3. **Save the File:**
   Save your program by selecting "Save" from the File menu or using the shortcut Ctrl+S (Windows) or Cmd+S (Mac).

4. **Run Your Program:**

     ○ If you're using IDLE, press F5 or select "Run Module" from the menu.

In VS Code, press Ctrl+Shift+B or use the terminal with the command:
python first_program.py

View the Output:
The output should display:

Hello, World!

What Did You Learn?

- **Syntax:** The rules of writing code in a programming language.
- **Function:** The print() function in Python outputs text to the console.
- **Execution:** Running code transforms it into actions performed by the computer.

Starting with a simple "Hello, World!" program might seem basic, but it introduces you to the core concepts of programming. From here, you can explore more complex topics, such as variables, control structures, and data manipulation, building a solid foundation for your programming journey.

Programming Languages Overview

Programming languages are the tools used to communicate instructions to computers. They vary widely in syntax, structure, and purpose, but all aim to translate human logic into machine-executable code. Understanding their types, popular options, and selection criteria is key to navigating the world of programming effectively.

Types of Programming Languages: Compiled vs. Interpreted

Programming languages are often categorized based on how they are executed by computers. Two primary types are **compiled** and **interpreted** languages.

Compiled Languages

A compiled language requires the code to be translated into machine code (binary) before execution. This translation is done using a compiler.

Key Characteristics:

- **Performance:** Compiled code runs faster because it is directly executed by the computer's CPU.
- **Error Detection:** The compiler catches many errors before the program runs.
- **Platform Dependency:** Compiled code is often platform-specific, meaning the binary may need recompilation for different systems.

Examples of Compiled Languages:

- **C:** Known for its speed and low-level capabilities, often used for system programming.
- **C++:** An extension of C with object-oriented features, widely used in game development and high-performance applications.
- **Rust:** A modern compiled language focusing on safety and concurrency.

Interpreted Languages

An interpreted language is executed line-by-line by an interpreter at runtime, without a separate compilation step.

Key Characteristics:

- **Flexibility:** Easy to test and debug as changes are immediately reflected during execution.
- **Portability:** Can often run on any platform with the appropriate interpreter installed.

- **Performance Trade-off:** Slower than compiled languages due to runtime interpretation.

Examples of Interpreted Languages:

- **Python:** Known for its simplicity and versatility, used in web development, AI, and data analysis.
- **JavaScript:** The language of the web, powering dynamic content and interactivity.
- **Ruby:** Focuses on developer happiness with a clean and intuitive syntax.

Hybrid Languages

Some languages, like Java, combine compilation and interpretation. Java code is compiled into an intermediate form called bytecode, which is then interpreted or compiled further by the Java Virtual Machine (JVM).

Popular Languages Today

With the vast array of programming languages available, some have emerged as industry standards due to their versatility, efficiency, and strong community support.

1. **Python**

    o **Strengths:**
        ■ Simple syntax and readability make it beginner-friendly.
        ■ Extensive libraries support fields like data science (NumPy, Pandas), machine learning (TensorFlow, PyTorch), and web development (Django, Flask).
    o **Use Cases:** AI/ML, web development, scripting, automation.

2. **JavaScript**

    o **Strengths:**
        ■ Essential for web development, as it runs directly in browsers.

- Paired with frameworks like React, Angular, and Vue for front-end, and Node.js for back-end.
  - **Use Cases:** Front-end and back-end web development, mobile apps (via React Native).

3. **Java**

- **Strengths:**
  - Write-once-run-anywhere capability through the JVM.
  - Strong performance and reliability, with a focus on enterprise applications.
  - **Use Cases:** Enterprise software, Android app development, web servers.

4. **C++**

- **Strengths:**
  - High performance and control over system resources.

- Rich support for object-oriented programming.
- ○ **Use Cases:** Game development, high-performance computing, embedded systems.

5. **C#**

  - ○ **Strengths:**
    - Developed by Microsoft, well-integrated with Windows applications and .NET.
    - Simplified syntax compared to C++.
  - ○ **Use Cases:** Game development (Unity), desktop applications, web applications.

6. **Swift**

  - ○ **Strengths:**
    - Designed by Apple for iOS and macOS applications.

- Modern and safe syntax with fast performance.
  - ○ **Use Cases:** Mobile app development for Apple platforms.
7. **Go (Golang)**

  - ○ **Strengths:**
    - Developed by Google, focuses on simplicity, concurrency, and scalability.
  - ○ **Use Cases:** Cloud computing, web servers, distributed systems.
8. **Rust**

  - ○ **Strengths:**
    - Prioritizes safety, especially in concurrent programming.
    - Growing popularity for its performance and security features.
  - ○ **Use Cases:** System programming, performance-critical applications.

Choosing the Right Language

Selecting the right programming language depends on your goals, project requirements, and personal preferences. Here are key considerations:

1. **Purpose of the Project:**

    - **Web Development:** JavaScript (front-end and back-end), Python, PHP.
    - **Mobile App Development:** Swift (iOS), Kotlin (Android).
    - **Data Science and AI:** Python, R.
    - **Game Development:** C++, C#, JavaScript.
    - **System Programming:** C, Rust.

2. **Ease of Learning:**

    - Beginners often start with Python due to its straightforward syntax.
    - Visual learners might prefer JavaScript to quickly see results in web browsers.

3. **Community and Ecosystem:**

   ○ Languages with active communities and abundant resources, like Python and JavaScript, are easier to learn and troubleshoot.

4. **Performance Needs:**

   ○ For high-performance applications, C++ or Rust might be necessary.
   ○ For less intensive tasks, Python or JavaScript is sufficient.

5. **Industry Standards:**

   ○ Certain fields have dominant languages. For instance:
      - **Web development:** JavaScript.
      - **Enterprise software:** Java.
      - **AI/ML:** Python.

6. **Job Market:**

   ○ Research demand in the job market for the language you are considering. Python and JavaScript are among the most sought-after.

7. **Longevity and Stability:**

   ○ Established languages like Java and C++ have stood the test of time, while emerging languages like Rust and Go promise modern capabilities.

Programming languages are the foundation of technology. Understanding their types, strengths, and applications allows developers to choose the best tool for their needs and adapt to the dynamic world of software development.

Core Programming Concepts

Core programming concepts form the foundation of any programming language. They encompass how data is stored, manipulated, and retrieved during the execution of a program. Mastering these basics is essential for writing functional and efficient code.

Variables and Data Types

Variables are named storage locations in a program that hold data values. A variable allows programmers to store, retrieve, and manipulate data dynamically during program execution.

1. Declaring Variables

The syntax for declaring a variable depends on the programming language. For example:

Python:
name = "Alice" # No explicit type declaration

Java:
int age = 25; // Type must be declared

2. Naming Variables

Variable names should be descriptive and adhere to the language's rules, such as starting with a letter or underscore and avoiding reserved keywords.

Examples of Good Variable Names:

- totalScore
- userName

Examples of Bad Variable Names:

- a, x, data1 (unless their purpose is clear).

3. Data Types

Data types define the kind of data a variable can hold. Common types include:

- **Numeric Types:**
    - **Integer:** Whole numbers (e.g., 5, -10).
    - **Float/Double:** Numbers with decimal points (e.g., 3.14, -0.001).
- **String:** A sequence of characters (e.g., "Hello", 'World').
- **Boolean:** True/False values used for logical operations.
- **Composite Types:**
    - **List/Array:** Ordered collections of values.
    - **Dictionary/Map:** Key-value pairs.
    - **Tuple:** Immutable collections.

4. Variable Scope

The **scope** of a variable determines where it can be accessed.

- **Local Variables:** Declared inside functions and accessible only within those functions.
- **Global Variables:** Declared outside any function and accessible throughout the program.

Operators and Expressions

Operators are symbols or keywords that perform operations on variables and values. When combined with variables or constants, they form **expressions**, which are evaluated to produce results.

1. Arithmetic Operators

Perform basic mathematical operations:

- Addition (+): x + y
- Subtraction (-): x - y
- Multiplication (*): x * y
- Division (/): x / y

- Modulus (%): x % y (remainder of division).

Example:

x = 10

y = 3

result = x % y # result is 1

2. Comparison Operators

Compare two values and return a Boolean result:

- Equal to (==): x == y
- Not equal to (!=): x != y
- Greater than (>): x > y
- Less than (<): x < y

Example:

x = 10

y = 5

print(x > y) # True

3. Logical Operators

Used for combining Boolean expressions:

- AND (and or &&): True if both conditions are true.
- OR (or or ||): True if at least one condition is true.
- NOT (not or !): Inverts the Boolean value.

Example:

x = 10

y = 5

print(x > 5 and y < 10) # True

4. Assignment Operators

Used to assign values to variables:

- Simple assignment (=): x = 10

Compound assignments (+=, -=, *=, /=):
x = 5

x += 3 # x is now 8

5. Expressions

An **expression** is any combination of variables, constants, and operators that the program can evaluate.

Example:

x = (10 + 5) * 2 # Evaluates to 30

Input and Output

Programs often interact with users or other systems through **input** and **output** (I/O) operations.

1. Input: Receiving Data

Input allows users to provide data during program execution. Most programming languages include built-in functions for input.

Python:
```
name = input("Enter your name: ")

print(f"Hello, {name}!")
```

Java:
```
 import java.util.Scanner;

Scanner scanner = new Scanner(System.in);

System.out.print("Enter your name: ");

String name = scanner.nextLine();

System.out.println("Hello, " + name + "!");
```

2. Output: Displaying Data

Output allows programs to display results or messages to users. Common output functions include:

Python:
```
 print("Hello, World!")
```

Java:
```
 System.out.println("Hello, World!");
```

3. Formatting Output

Most programming languages allow output to be formatted for readability.
 Example in Python:

name = "Alice"

score = 95.5

```
print(f"{name} scored {score:.2f} on the test.")
# Outputs: Alice scored 95.50 on the test.
```

4. File I/O

In addition to user input, programs can read from and write to files.

Reading a File (Python):
```
with open("example.txt", "r") as file:

    data = file.read()

print(data)
```

Writing to a File (Python):
```
with open("example.txt", "w") as file:

    file.write("Hello, File!")
```

Summary

Understanding variables, data types, operators, expressions, and I/O operations is foundational to programming. These concepts enable developers to:

- Store and manipulate data dynamically.
- Perform calculations and logical operations.
- Interact with users and external systems through inputs and outputs.

Control Flow

Control flow refers to the order in which individual statements, instructions, or function calls are executed in a program. By using conditional statements and loops, programmers can dictate complex decision-making and repetitive tasks. Mastering control flow is key to creating dynamic and efficient programs.

Conditional Statements: If, Else, and Switch

Conditional statements allow a program to execute certain blocks of code only when specific conditions are met.

1. If Statement

The **if** statement executes a block of code when a condition evaluates to true.

Syntax:

if condition:

    # code to execute if condition is true

Example in Python:

age = 20

if age >= 18:

    print("You are eligible to vote.")

Example in Java:

int age = 20;

if (age >= 18) {

    System.out.println("You are eligible to vote.");

}

2. If-Else Statement

The **if-else** statement provides an alternative block of code if the condition is false.

Syntax:

if condition:

    # code if condition is true

else:

    # code if condition is false

Example:

age = 16

if age >= 18:

    print("You are eligible to vote.")

else:

   print("You are not eligible to vote.")

3. Else If (Elif) Statement

The **else if** (Python: elif) statement allows checking multiple conditions sequentially.

Syntax:

if condition1:

   # code if condition1 is true

elif condition2:

   # code if condition2 is true

else:

   # code if none of the conditions are true

Example in Python:

score = 85

if score >= 90:

   print("Grade: A")

elif score >= 75:

   print("Grade: B")

else:

   print("Grade: C")

4. Switch Statement

The **switch** statement simplifies handling multiple conditions, especially when checking a single variable against various values.
Note: Python lacks a built-in switch statement but offers match-case in newer versions.

Syntax in Java:

int day = 3;

```
switch (day) {

    case 1:

        System.out.println("Monday");

        break;

    case 2:

        System.out.println("Tuesday");

        break;

    case 3:

        System.out.println("Wednesday");

        break;

    default:

        System.out.println("Invalid day");

}
```

Loops: For, While, and Do-While

Loops allow repeating a block of code as long as a condition is met. They are essential for tasks like iterating over data or automating repetitive processes.

1. For Loop

A **for** loop is used when the number of iterations is known beforehand.

Syntax in Python:

```python
for variable in iterable:

    # code to execute in each iteration
```

Example in Python:

```python
for i in range(5):  # Loops from 0 to 4

    print(i)
```

Syntax in Java:

```
for (initialization; condition; update) {

    // code to execute

}
```

Example in Java:

```java
for (int i = 0; i < 5; i++) {

    System.out.println(i);

}
```

2. While Loop

A **while** loop executes as long as the condition is true.

Syntax in Python:

```python
while condition:

    # code to execute
```

Example:

i = 0

while i < 5:

   print(i)

   i += 1

Syntax in Java:

while (condition) {

   // code to execute

}

3. Do-While Loop

The **do-while** loop guarantees at least one execution of the loop body since the condition is checked after the loop runs.

Syntax in Java:

```
do {

    // code to execute

} while (condition);
```

Example in Java:

```
int i = 0;

do {

    System.out.println(i);

    i++;

} while (i < 5);
```

Breaking and Continuing Loops

1. Break Statement

The break statement exits the loop immediately, regardless of the loop condition.

Example in Python:

```python
for i in range(10):
    if i == 5:
        break
    print(i)
# Output: 0, 1, 2, 3, 4
```

Example in Java:

```java
for (int i = 0; i < 10; i++) {
    if (i == 5) {
        break;
    }
    System.out.println(i);
```

}

2. Continue Statement

The continue statement skips the current iteration and moves to the next one.

Example in Python:

```python
for i in range(10):
    if i % 2 == 0:  # Skip even numbers
        continue
    print(i)
# Output: 1, 3, 5, 7, 9
```

Example in Java:

```java
for (int i = 0; i < 10; i++) {
    if (i % 2 == 0) {
```

```
    continue;

  }

  System.out.println(i);

}
```

3. Nested Loops with Break and Continue

Loops can be nested, and break or continue can be used for the inner or outer loops.

- **Break with a label (Java):** Allows breaking from a specific loop.

```
outerLoop:

for (int i = 0; i < 3; i++) {

  for (int j = 0; j < 3; j++) {

    if (j == 2) break outerLoop;

    System.out.println("i: " + i + ", j: " + j);

  }
```

}

Summary

Control flow structures like conditional statements and loops enable programs to make decisions and perform repetitive tasks efficiently. Key points to remember:

- Use **if-else** and **switch** for branching logic.
- Choose **for, while**, or **do-while** loops based on the problem's requirements.
- Use break and continue to control loop execution.

Functions and Modular Programming

Functions and modular programming are essential concepts in programming that promote code reuse, readability, and maintainability. By breaking a program into smaller, manageable units, developers can focus on individual components, make debugging easier, and create reusable building blocks for larger applications.

Defining and Calling Functions

What Are Functions?

A **function** is a self-contained block of code that performs a specific task. It takes inputs (optional), processes them, and may return an output.

Advantages of Using Functions:

- **Reusability**: Functions can be reused in multiple places, reducing code duplication.
- **Modularity**: Divides programs into smaller, manageable sections.
- **Maintainability**: Easier to debug and modify individual functions.
- **Readability**: Improves the clarity of code by abstracting complex operations.

Defining a Function

To define a function, you typically specify:

1. A **name** for the function.
2. A set of **parameters** (optional).
3. A **body** containing the operations.
4. A **return statement** (optional) for output.

Example in Python:

```python
def greet(name):

    """Function to greet a user by name."""

    print(f"Hello, {name}!")
```

Example in Java:

```java
void greet(String name) {

    System.out.println("Hello, " + name + "!");

}
```

Calling a Function

Calling a function executes its code. You invoke it by using its name and passing required arguments.

Example in Python:

```python
greet("Alice")
```

Output: Hello, Alice!

Example in Java:

greet("Alice");

// Output: Hello, Alice!

Parameters and Return Values

Functions often require inputs (parameters) and produce outputs (return values).

Parameters

Parameters allow passing data into functions for processing. They are defined in the function signature and used within the function body.

Types of Parameters:

1. **Positional Parameters**: Matched based on their position during function call.
2. **Default Parameters**: Provide default values if not explicitly passed.
3. **Keyword Arguments** (Python-specific): Specify parameters by name.

Example in Python:

```python
def add(a, b=5):

    return a + b



print(add(3))      # Uses default b=5, Output: 8

print(add(3, 7))   # Overrides default b, Output: 10
```

Example in Java:

```java
int add(int a, int b) {

    return a + b;
```

```
}
```

System.out.println(add(3, 7)); // Output: 10

Return Values

A **return value** is the output of a function. It is specified using the return keyword.

Example in Python:

```python
def square(x):

    return x * x


result = square(4)

print(result)  # Output: 16
```

Example in Java:

```
int square(int x) {

    return x * x;

}
```

```
int result = square(4);

System.out.println(result);  // Output: 16
```

Scope and Lifetime of Variables

Scope refers to the part of a program where a variable is accessible. **Lifetime** is the duration for which the variable exists during execution.

Types of Scope

1. **Global Scope**:

   ○ Variables declared outside functions.

- ○ Accessible throughout the program.
- ○ Overuse can lead to bugs and reduced modularity.

Example in Python:

```
x = 10  # Global variable


def show_value():

  print(x)



show_value()  # Output: 10
```

2. **Local Scope**:

- ○ Variables declared inside a function.
- ○ Accessible only within that function.
- ○ Protects variables from unintentional modification.

Example:

```
def demo():

  y = 5  # Local variable

  print(y)


demo()  # Output: 5

# print(y)  # Error: y is not defined
```

Lifetime of Variables

- **Local variables** exist only during the function's execution and are destroyed afterward.
- **Global variables** persist throughout the program's execution unless explicitly deleted.

Modular Design Principles

Modular programming involves dividing a program into independent, reusable modules or functions that work together to solve a problem.

Benefits of Modular Design

1. **Reusability**: Modules can be reused in different programs or parts of the same program.
2. **Ease of Debugging**: Problems can be isolated to specific modules.
3. **Maintainability**: Easier to modify and update without affecting the entire program.
4. **Scalability**: Facilitates the addition of new features without rewriting existing code.

Principles of Modular Design

1. **Cohesion:**

- A module should focus on a single task or responsibility.
- High cohesion improves readability and maintainability.

2. **Coupling**:

- Modules should be loosely coupled, meaning they have minimal dependencies on each other.
- Reduces the impact of changes in one module on others.

3. **Encapsulation**:

- Hide implementation details and expose only necessary functionalities through public interfaces.

4. **Abstraction**:

- Define clear interfaces for modules to communicate without revealing internal details.

Examples of Modular Design

1. Python Modular Programming:

- Split the program into files (modules) and reuse them.

```python
# math_utils.py

def add(a, b):
    return a + b
```

```python
# main.py

from math_utils import add

print(add(2, 3))  # Output: 5
```

2. Java Modular Programming:

- Use classes and packages to organize code.

```java
// MathUtils.java

public class MathUtils {

    public static int add(int a, int b) {

        return a + b;

    }

}
```

```java
// Main.java

public class Main {

    public static void main(String[] args) {

        System.out.println(MathUtils.add(2, 3));  // Output: 5

    }

}
```

Summary

Functions and modular programming are the backbone of structured and efficient software development. Key takeaways include:

1. **Functions**: Reusable blocks of code that simplify complex tasks.
2. **Parameters and Return Values**: Facilitate input/output for functions.
3. **Scope and Lifetime**: Manage variable accessibility and persistence.
4. **Modular Design Principles**: Promote clean, maintainable, and scalable code.

Data Structures

Data structures are fundamental components of computer programming, organizing and storing data efficiently for effective access, modification, and management. The choice of a data structure impacts program performance and determines how data operations are performed.

Arrays and Lists

Arrays

An **array** is a linear data structure consisting of elements of the same type, stored in contiguous memory locations. Each element is accessed using an index.

Key Features:

- **Fixed Size**: Arrays have a predefined size that cannot be changed dynamically.
- **Efficient Indexing**: Accessing an element by index is an $O(1)O(1)$ operation.
- **Homogeneous Elements**: All elements are of the same data type.

Example in Python:

arr = [10, 20, 30, 40] # Array-like list

print(arr[2]) # Output: 30

Example in Java:

int[] arr = {10, 20, 30, 40};

System.out.println(arr[2]); // Output: 30

Applications:

- Storing fixed collections of data.

- Implementing matrices for mathematical computations.

Lists

A **list** is a dynamic data structure that allows the storage of elements, which may be of different types (e.g., in Python). Lists can grow or shrink in size as needed.

Features:

- **Dynamic Size**: No need to specify size beforehand.
- **Flexible Element Types**: In Python, lists can hold elements of different data types.
- **Versatility**: Many built-in operations for manipulation.

Example in Python:

lst = [1, "hello", 3.14]

lst.append("new")

print(lst) # Output: [1, 'hello', 3.14, 'new']

Stacks, Queues, and Deques

Stacks

A **stack** is a linear data structure that follows the **Last In, First Out (LIFO)** principle. The last element added is the first to be removed.

Operations:

1. **Push**: Add an element to the top.
2. **Pop**: Remove and return the top element.
3. **Peek/Top**: View the top element without removing it.

Example in Python:

```
stack = []

stack.append(10)  # Push
```

```
stack.append(20)

print(stack.pop())  # Pop, Output: 20
```

Applications:

- Function call management (call stack).
- Undo/redo functionality in text editors.

Queues

A **queue** is a linear data structure following the **First In, First Out (FIFO)** principle. The first element added is the first to be removed.

Operations:

1. **Enqueue**: Add an element to the end.
2. **Dequeue**: Remove and return the front element.

Example in Python:

```
from collections import deque
```

```
queue = deque()

queue.append(10)  # Enqueue

queue.append(20)

print(queue.popleft())  # Dequeue, Output: 10
```

Applications:

- Task scheduling.
- Breadth-first search (BFS) in graphs.

Deques

A **deque** (double-ended queue) is a generalized version of a queue that allows elements to be added or removed from both ends.

Example in Python:

```
from collections import deque
```

87

dq = deque()

dq.append(10) # Add to the right

dq.appendleft(20) # Add to the left

print(dq.pop()) # Remove from the right,
Output: 10

Applications:

- Sliding window problems.
- Palindrome checking.

Dictionaries and Hash Tables

Dictionaries

A **dictionary** is a collection of key-value pairs where each key maps to a value. Dictionaries allow fast lookups and updates based on keys.

Example in Python:

```
person = {"name": "Alice", "age": 30}

print(person["name"])  # Output: Alice
```

Applications:

- Storing configurations.
- Representing sparse data.

Hash Tables

A **hash table** is a data structure that maps keys to values using a hash function. It enables $O(1)$ average-time complexity for lookups, insertions, and deletions.

Key Features:

- Uses a hash function to compute an index.
- Handles collisions using chaining or open addressing.

Example in Python (dict as hash table):

hash_table = {}

hash_table["key1"] = "value1"

print(hash_table["key1"]) # Output: value1

Applications:

- Caching.
- Implementing sets and dictionaries.

Trees and Graphs

Trees

A **tree** is a hierarchical data structure where each node has one parent (except the root) and zero or more children.

Binary Trees: A binary tree is a tree where each node has at most two children.

Binary Search Tree (BST): A BST is a binary tree where:

- Left child << Parent
- Right child >> Parent

Example in Python:

```python
class Node:

    def __init__(self, value):

        self.value = value

        self.left = None

        self.right = None


root = Node(10)

root.left = Node(5)

root.right = Node(20)
```

Applications:

- Hierarchical data representation (e.g., file systems).
- Searching and sorting algorithms.

Graphs

A **graph** is a collection of nodes (vertices) connected by edges. Graphs may be:

1. **Directed** or **Undirected**.
2. **Weighted** or **Unweighted**.

Graph Representation:

1. **Adjacency List**:
   - Each node points to a list of its neighbors.
2. **Adjacency Matrix**:
   - A 2D array where cell [i][j][i][j] indicates the presence of an edge between nodes ii and jj.

Example in Python (Adjacency List):

graph = {

```
"A": ["B", "C"],

"B": ["A", "D"],

"C": ["A", "D"],

"D": ["B", "C"]

}
```

Applications:

- Social networks.
- Pathfinding algorithms (e.g., Dijkstra's).

Summary

Understanding and using data structures effectively is crucial for solving computational problems efficiently. Key takeaways:

1. **Arrays and Lists**: Best for ordered collections of data.

2. **Stacks, Queues, and Deques**: Manage data with specific insertion/removal rules.
3. **Dictionaries and Hash Tables**: Provide fast lookups and key-value mappings.
4. **Trees and Graphs**: Handle hierarchical and networked data.

Choosing the right data structure depends on the specific requirements of the application and the operations needed.

Object-Oriented Programming (OOP)

Object-Oriented Programming (OOP) is a programming paradigm that organizes software design around **objects**, which represent real-world entities. These objects encapsulate both **data** (attributes) and **behaviors** (methods), making it easier to model, understand, and manipulate complex systems. OOP promotes modularity, reusability, and scalability, making it a cornerstone of modern software development.

Classes and Objects

What Are Classes?

A **class** is a blueprint for creating objects. It defines the properties (attributes) and behaviors (methods) that objects created from the class will have.

Syntax in Python:

```python
class Person:

    def __init__(self, name, age):  # Constructor method
        self.name = name

        self.age = age


    def greet(self):

        print(f"Hello, my name is {self.name}.")
```

Syntax in Java:

```java
class Person {
```

```
    String name;

    int age;


    Person(String name, int age) {  // Constructor

        this.name = name;

        this.age = age;

    }


    void greet() {

        System.out.println("Hello, my name is " +
name + ".");

    }

}
```

What Are Objects?

An **object** is an instance of a class. Each object has its own state (data) and can perform actions defined by the class.

Example in Python:

Creating an object

person1 = Person("Alice", 30)

person1.greet() # Output: Hello, my name is Alice.

Example in Java:

Person person1 = new Person("Alice", 30);

person1.greet(); // Output: Hello, my name is Alice.

Inheritance and Polymorphism

Inheritance

Inheritance allows a class (child or subclass) to inherit properties and methods from another class (parent or superclass). This promotes code reuse and hierarchy.

Example in Python:

```python
class Employee(Person):  # Employee inherits from Person

    def __init__(self, name, age, position):

        super().__init__(name, age)

        self.position = position


    def work(self):

        print(f"{self.name} is working as a {self.position}.")
```

Example in Java:

```java
class Employee extends Person {
```

```
    String position;


    Employee(String name, int age, String position) {

        super(name, age);  // Call to parent constructor

        this.position = position;

    }


    void work() {

        System.out.println(name + " is working as a " + position + ".");

    }

}
```

Polymorphism

Polymorphism allows objects of different classes to be treated as objects of a common superclass, with the correct method being called based on the object's actual type.

Method Overriding: A subclass can redefine a method from its superclass.

Example in Python:

```python
class Manager(Employee):

    def work(self):

        print(f"{self.name} is managing the team.")
```

Example in Java:

```java
class Manager extends Employee {

    Manager(String name, int age, String position)
{

        super(name, age, position);

    }
```

```
@Override

void work() {

    System.out.println(name + " is managing
the team.");

    }

}
```

Encapsulation and Abstraction

Encapsulation

Encapsulation is the bundling of data (attributes) and methods (functions) into a single unit (class) and restricting access to some components.

Access Modifiers:

- **Public**: Accessible from anywhere.
- **Protected**: Accessible within the same package or by subclasses.

- **Private**: Accessible only within the class.

Example in Python:

```python
class BankAccount:

    def __init__(self, account_holder, balance):

        self.account_holder = account_holder  # Public attribute

        self.__balance = balance  # Private attribute


    def deposit(self, amount):

        self.__balance += amount


    def get_balance(self):

        return self.__balance
```

Example in Java:

```
class BankAccount {

    public String accountHolder;

    private double balance;


    BankAccount(String accountHolder, double
balance) {

        this.accountHolder = accountHolder;

        this.balance = balance;

    }


    void deposit(double amount) {

        balance += amount;

    }


    double getBalance() {
```

```
    return balance;

  }

}
```

Abstraction

Abstraction hides the implementation details of a class and only exposes the essential functionalities.

Abstract Classes: Abstract classes cannot be instantiated directly and often contain abstract methods (methods without a body).

Example in Python:

```python
from abc import ABC, abstractmethod


class Animal(ABC):

  @abstractmethod
```

```python
    def make_sound(self):

        pass


class Dog(Animal):

    def make_sound(self):

        print("Bark!")
```

Example in Java:

```java
abstract class Animal {

    abstract void makeSound();

}


class Dog extends Animal {

    @Override

    void makeSound() {
```

```
System.out.println("Bark!");

    }

}
```

Design Patterns in OOP

Design patterns are proven solutions to common software design problems. They promote best practices in OOP.

1. Singleton Pattern

Ensures that a class has only one instance and provides a global point of access to it.

Example in Python:

```python
class Singleton:

    _instance = None


    @staticmethod
```

```
def get_instance():

    if Singleton._instance is None:

        Singleton._instance = Singleton()

    return Singleton._instance
```

Example in Java:

```
class Singleton {

    private static Singleton instance;


    private Singleton() {}


    public static Singleton getInstance() {

        if (instance == null) {

            instance = new Singleton();

        }
```

```
        return instance;

    }

}
```

---

2. Factory Pattern

Creates objects without specifying the exact class of object that will be created.

Example in Python:

```python
class Shape:

    def draw(self):

        pass


class Circle(Shape):

    def draw(self):

        print("Drawing Circle")
```

```
class ShapeFactory:

    @staticmethod

    def get_shape(shape_type):

        if shape_type == "circle":

            return Circle()
```

---

3. Observer Pattern

Defines a dependency between objects so that when one object changes state, its dependents are notified.

Summary

Object-Oriented Programming (OOP) offers a robust framework for designing and building scalable, reusable, and maintainable applications. Key concepts include:

1. **Classes and Objects**: The building blocks of OOP.
2. **Inheritance and Polymorphism**: Promote code reuse and flexibility.
3. **Encapsulation and Abstraction**: Enhance security and hide implementation details.
4. **Design Patterns**: Provide structured solutions to recurring design challenges.

Error Handling and Debugging

Error handling and debugging are crucial skills in programming, as they enable developers to identify, isolate, and resolve issues in code. Errors are inevitable in programming, but how they are handled can greatly affect the reliability and user experience of an application. Proper error handling ensures that the program can continue functioning smoothly even in the face of unexpected situations, while debugging helps identify and fix issues during development.

Types of Errors: Syntax, Runtime, and Logical

1. Syntax Errors

A **syntax error** occurs when the programmer writes code that does not conform to the rules or grammar of the programming language. This type of error is detected by the compiler or interpreter before the program runs. It prevents the program from executing until the issue is fixed.

Common causes of syntax errors:

- Missing parentheses or braces.
- Incorrect variable names or undeclared variables.
- Misuse of operators or keywords.
- Incorrect indentation (in languages like Python, where indentation is syntactically important).

Example in Python:

```
print("Hello, world!"  # Missing closing
parenthesis
```

Example in Java:

System.out.println("Hello, world!"; // Missing closing parenthesis and semicolon

Fix:

- Ensure correct syntax, such as closing parentheses or braces.

---

2. Runtime Errors

A **runtime error** occurs while the program is running, causing it to crash or behave unexpectedly. These errors happen during the program's execution, often as a result of invalid operations or inputs.

Common causes of runtime errors:

- Dividing by zero.
- Accessing an array index that is out of bounds.

- Null pointer dereference (in languages like Java or C++).
- Incorrect resource allocation, such as opening files that do not exist.

Example in Python:

x = 10 / 0 # Division by zero

Example in Java:

int[] arr = {1, 2, 3};

System.out.println(arr[5]); // Array index out of bounds

Fix:

- Add checks or conditionals to handle cases that could cause runtime failures, such as verifying the divisor is not zero or ensuring array indices are within bounds.

---

3. Logical Errors

A **logical error** occurs when the program runs without crashing, but the output or behavior is incorrect. These errors are often the hardest to identify because the program compiles and runs successfully but produces incorrect results due to flawed logic.

Common causes of logical errors:

- Incorrect algorithm or formula.
- Incorrect use of conditional statements.
- Flawed flow of control or improper order of operations.

Example in Python:

```python
def add(a, b):

    return a - b  # Should be addition, not subtraction


result = add(5, 3)
```

print(result) # Output: 2 instead of 8

Example in Java:

```
int add(int a, int b) {

    return a - b;  // Incorrect operation

}
```

```
System.out.println(add(5, 3));  // Output: 2
instead of 8
```

Fix:

- Use test cases and validate expected results. Logical errors typically require reviewing and rethinking the algorithm or flow of control in the code.

Exception Handling

Exception handling allows programmers to manage errors gracefully without crashing the program. Exceptions are runtime errors that can be "caught" and handled using special constructs in many programming languages. By handling exceptions, programs can recover from unexpected situations and continue functioning.

1. What is an Exception?

An **exception** is an abnormal condition that disrupts the normal flow of program execution. It can be caused by a variety of reasons such as invalid user input, missing files, or network issues. In most programming languages, exceptions are represented as objects that contain information about the error, such as its type, message, and location.

2. Exception Handling Mechanism

In many programming languages, exception handling is done using a try, except, catch, or finally block (depending on the language).

Python:

try:

   x = 10 / 0 # Potential runtime error (division by zero)

except ZeroDivisionError as e:

   print("Error:", e) # Handle the exception

finally:

   print("This block always runs, even if an exception occurs.")

Java:

```
try {

    int[] arr = {1, 2, 3};

    System.out.println(arr[5]);  // Array index out of bounds

} catch (ArrayIndexOutOfBoundsException e) {
```

```
System.out.println("Error: " +
e.getMessage());

} finally {

System.out.println("This block always runs.");

}
```

3. Types of Exceptions

1. **Checked Exceptions (Java)**: Exceptions that must be explicitly handled or declared using throws in Java. Examples include IOException and SQLException.
2. **Unchecked Exceptions**: These exceptions do not need to be explicitly handled. They usually occur due to programming errors, such as NullPointerException or ArithmeticException.
3. **Custom Exceptions**: Programmers can define their own exception types to represent specific error conditions in the application.

Example in Python:

```python
class CustomError(Exception):

    def __init__(self, message):

        self.message = message

        super().__init__(self.message)


try:

    raise CustomError("This is a custom exception.")

except CustomError as e:

    print("Caught:", e)
```

4. Best Practices for Exception Handling

- **Catch Specific Exceptions**: Avoid using a generic catch or except for all exceptions. Catch only the exceptions you expect and know how to handle.

- **Log Exceptions**: Always log exceptions with detailed information, such as the stack trace, so that the root cause can be identified.
- **Fail Gracefully**: Ensure that the application does not crash when an exception occurs. Instead, display user-friendly error messages or attempt to recover from the error.
- **Clean-up Resources**: Use finally or equivalent constructs to ensure that resources (files, network connections, etc.) are closed or released, even if an exception occurs.

Debugging Tools and Techniques

Debugging is the process of identifying and fixing errors in a program. There are various tools and techniques available to assist in the debugging process.

1. Print-Based Debugging

A simple and effective method to understand what is happening inside a program is to add print statements at various points to track variable values, execution flow, and program state.

Example in Python:

```
def calculate_area(radius):

    print("Radius:", radius)

    area = 3.14 * radius * radius

    print("Area:", area)

    return area


calculate_area(5)
```

2. Breakpoints and Step-Through Debugging

123

Modern Integrated Development Environments (IDEs) provide powerful debugging features, such as **breakpoints** and **step-through debugging**. A breakpoint is a marker in the code where the program will pause during execution, allowing the developer to inspect the program's state at that point.

Key Debugging Features:

- **Set Breakpoints**: Pause the program execution at a specific line of code.
- **Step Into**: Execute code line by line and inspect function calls.
- **Step Over**: Skip over function calls and execute the rest of the code.
- **Watch Variables**: Monitor the value of specific variables as the program executes.

3. Using a Debugger

A **debugger** is a tool that helps identify bugs by allowing step-by-step execution of the code, examining variable states, and catching exceptions.

Example Tools:

- **GDB**: GNU Debugger, used for debugging C/C++ programs.
- **PDB**: Python Debugger, a tool for Python that provides command-line debugging features.
- **IDE Debuggers**: Most IDEs (like Visual Studio, PyCharm, or Eclipse) come with built-in debuggers that integrate seamlessly with the code.

4. Unit Testing

Unit testing involves writing tests for individual parts of your code, ensuring that each component functions as expected. Automated testing frameworks can help identify bugs early in the development cycle.

Example in Python (using unittest):

```
import unittest
```

```
def add(a, b):

    return a + b


class TestMathFunctions(unittest.TestCase):

    def test_add(self):

        self.assertEqual(add(3, 5), 8)


if __name__ == "__main__":

    unittest.main()
```

Summary

Effective error handling and debugging are essential for building reliable software. Key points to remember include:

1. **Types of Errors**:

- ○ **Syntax Errors**: Detected before the program runs.
- ○ **Runtime Errors**: Occur during program execution.
- ○ **Logical Errors**: The program runs but produces incorrect results.

2. **Exception Handling**: Use try, except, and custom exceptions to handle errors gracefully.

3. **Debugging Techniques**: Utilize print statements, breakpoints, and debuggers to identify and fix bugs.

4. **Best Practices**: Catch specific exceptions, log errors, and clean up resources to improve the reliability of your applications.

By mastering these techniques, developers can ensure that their applications run smoothly and are more resilient to unexpected issues.

File Handling and I/O

File handling and input/output (I/O) operations are fundamental tasks in programming, allowing applications to interact with external data. File handling enables reading from and writing to files, which is critical for persistent storage, logging, data processing, and communication with external systems. Understanding how to effectively handle files and I/O operations is a core skill for programmers working on real-world applications.

Working with Files

What is File Handling?

File handling refers to the process of working with files on the file system, including performing operations such as:

- **Opening** a file to access its contents.
- **Reading** from a file to retrieve data.
- **Writing** to a file to save data.
- **Closing** a file to release system resources.

Files can be of various types, such as **text files**, **binary files**, and **CSV files**, each requiring different methods of reading and writing.

Opening a File

Before interacting with a file, it must be opened. Most programming languages provide functions or classes to handle file opening and closing. When a file is opened, a handle is created, which allows the program to perform operations on the file.

- **Python**: Uses the built-in open() function.
- **Java**: Uses classes like File, FileReader, and FileWriter.

Syntax in Python:

```
file = open("example.txt", "r")  # Open file for reading (r)
```

Syntax in Java:

import java.io.File;

import java.io.FileReader;

import java.io.IOException;

File file = new File("example.txt");

FileReader fr = new FileReader(file);

The file can be opened in different modes:

- "r": Read (default mode).
- "w": Write (creates or truncates the file).
- "a": Append (adds data to the end of the file).
- "rb", "wb": Binary read/write mode.

Closing a File

After completing file operations, it is important to **close** the file to release system resources and ensure that all data is written properly.

- **Python**: file.close()
- **Java**: fr.close()

In Python, it's often recommended to use the with statement to automatically close the file after the operations are complete, ensuring that resources are properly released even in the event of an error.

Example in Python:

with open("example.txt", "r") as file:

   content = file.read()

File is automatically closed after this block

Example in Java (using try-with-resources for automatic resource management):

```
try (FileReader fr = new
FileReader("example.txt")) {

    // Read data here

} catch (IOException e) {

    e.printStackTrace();

}

// File is automatically closed
```

Reading and Writing Data

Reading from Files

The method for reading data depends on the file type and the desired content format.

Reading Text Files:

- **Python**: You can use read(), readline(), or readlines() methods.
- **Java**: Use FileReader, BufferedReader, or Scanner for reading text files.

Python Example (Reading entire file):

```python
with open("example.txt", "r") as file:

    content = file.read()  # Reads the entire file

    print(content)
```

Python Example (Reading line by line):

```python
with open("example.txt", "r") as file:

    for line in file:

        print(line.strip())  # Strips newline
characters
```

Java Example (Using BufferedReader):

```java
import java.io.*;
```

```
try (BufferedReader br = new
BufferedReader(new
FileReader("example.txt"))) {

    String line;

    while ((line = br.readLine()) != null) {

        System.out.println(line);

    }

} catch (IOException e) {

    e.printStackTrace();

}
```

Writing to Files

Writing to files allows you to store data persistently. You can either overwrite or append data based on the file mode used.

Python Example (Writing to a file):

```python
with open("example.txt", "w") as file:

    file.write("Hello, World!")
```

Python Example (Appending to a file):

```python
with open("example.txt", "a") as file:

    file.write("\nThis is an appended line.")
```

Java Example (Using FileWriter):

```java
import java.io.*;


try (FileWriter writer = new
FileWriter("example.txt")) {

    writer.write("Hello, World!");

} catch (IOException e) {

    e.printStackTrace();
```

```
}
```

Java Example (Appending to a file):

import java.io.*;

```
try (FileWriter writer = new
FileWriter("example.txt", true)) {

    writer.write("\nThis is an appended line.");

} catch (IOException e) {

    e.printStackTrace();

}
```

Binary File Operations

Binary files are used for storing data in a format that is not human-readable, such as images, audio, or structured data. Reading and writing binary files requires working with byte-oriented operations.

- **Python**: Use "rb" (read binary) or "wb" (write binary) modes.
- **Java**: Use FileInputStream and FileOutputStream.

Python Example (Reading binary file):

```python
with open("image.jpg", "rb") as file:

    content = file.read()  # Read as binary data

    # Process content as needed
```

Java Example (Reading binary file):

```java
import java.io.*;


try (FileInputStream fis = new
FileInputStream("image.jpg")) {

    int byteData;
```

```
while ((byteData = fis.read()) != -1) {

    System.out.print(byteData + " ");

  }

} catch (IOException e) {

  e.printStackTrace();

}
```

File Formats and Parsing

Common File Formats

Understanding different file formats and how to parse them is essential for dealing with external data sources.

1. **Text Files**: Simple files containing human-readable characters, such as .txt files. These files can be read line by line or as a whole.
2. **CSV (Comma-Separated Values)**: A text format used for storing tabular data. Each

line represents a record, and columns are separated by commas or other delimiters.

3. **JSON (JavaScript Object Notation)**: A lightweight data interchange format used for representing structured data as key-value pairs. It is commonly used in web applications and APIs.

4. **XML (eXtensible Markup Language)**: A markup language used for encoding documents in a format that is both human-readable and machine-readable.

5. **Binary Formats**: Used for more efficient data storage, such as .jpg, .png, .mp3, or custom binary formats.

Parsing CSV Files

CSV files are commonly used for storing tabular data. Many programming languages provide libraries to parse CSV files efficiently.

Python Example (Using csv module):

```
import csv
```

```python
with open("data.csv", "r") as file:

    reader = csv.reader(file)

    for row in reader:

        print(row)  # Each row is a list of column values
```

Java Example (Using CSVReader from OpenCSV library):

```java
import com.opencsv.CSVReader;

import java.io.*;

import java.util.List;


try (CSVReader reader = new CSVReader(new FileReader("data.csv"))) {

    List<String[]> records = reader.readAll();

    for (String[] record : records) {
```

```
    System.out.println(String.join(", ", record));
// Print each record

  }

} catch (IOException e) {

  e.printStackTrace();

}
```

Parsing JSON Files

JSON is a widely used data format for APIs and web services. It can easily be parsed into structured data like dictionaries (Python) or maps (Java).

Python Example (Using json module):

```python
import json


with open("data.json", "r") as file:
```

data = json.load(file) # Parse JSON into a Python dictionary

print(data)

Java Example (Using Jackson library):

import com.fasterxml.jackson.databind.ObjectMapper;

import java.io.File;

import java.io.IOException;

ObjectMapper objectMapper = new ObjectMapper();

try {

    MyData data = objectMapper.readValue(new File("data.json"), MyData.class);

    System.out.println(data);

```
} catch (IOException e) {

    e.printStackTrace();

}
```

Parsing XML Files

XML is a flexible markup language commonly used for storing data in a hierarchical format. In Java, you can use libraries like DOM, SAX, or JAXP to parse XML files.

Python Example (Using xml.etree.ElementTree):

```python
import xml.etree.ElementTree as ET


tree = ET.parse("data.xml")
root = tree.getroot()
```

```
for child in root:

    print(child.tag, child.text)
```

Java Example (Using DOM parser):

```
import org.w3c.dom.*;

import javax.xml.parsers.*;


File xmlFile = new File("data.xml");

DocumentBuilderFactory dbFactory =
DocumentBuilderFactory.newInstance();

DocumentBuilder dBuilder =
dbFactory.newDocumentBuilder();

Document doc = dBuilder.parse(xmlFile);

doc.getDocumentElement().normalize();
```

```
NodeList nList =
doc.getElementsByTagName("element");


for (int i =


0; i < nList.getLength(); i++) { Node node =
nList.item(i); if (node.getNodeType() ==
Node.ELEMENT_NODE) { Element element =
(Element) node; System.out.println("Element: "
+ element.getTextContent()); } }
```

Summary

File handling and I/O operations are essential for reading and writing data in a program. Key concepts include:

1. **Opening and Closing Files**: Essential for accessing and releasing file resources.
2. **Reading and Writing Data**: Use appropriate methods to handle different file types, whether text or binary.

3. **File Formats**: Understand common formats such as CSV, JSON, XML, and how to parse them using libraries.

4. **Binary File Operations**: For efficient handling of non-human-readable data.

Introduction to Algorithms

Algorithms are fundamental to computer science and programming, serving as the backbone of efficient problem-solving. An algorithm is a step-by-step procedure or set of rules that defines how to solve a problem or perform a task. Whether you're sorting a list, finding the shortest path between two points, or searching for an element in a collection, algorithms guide how these tasks are executed in the most efficient and effective way possible. Understanding algorithms is crucial for writing high-performance software and optimizing computational tasks.

What is an Algorithm?

At its core, an **algorithm** is a sequence of well-defined instructions that transforms input into output. It takes an initial state, processes input through a series of steps, and produces the desired result. The key characteristics of a good algorithm include:

- **Finiteness**: An algorithm must eventually terminate after a finite number of steps.
- **Definiteness**: Every step of the algorithm must be precisely defined, leaving no ambiguity.
- **Input**: The algorithm must take input (data) to process.
- **Output**: The algorithm must produce an output that solves the problem.
- **Effectiveness**: The steps must be simple enough to be carried out, typically by a computer, within finite time and resources.

A well-designed algorithm can significantly improve the performance of an application, reducing the amount of time or memory required to complete a task.

Example of a simple algorithm (Finding the largest number in a list):

1. Start with an empty list or array.
2. Set the first element of the list as the current largest.
3. For each subsequent element, compare it with the current largest.
    o If the element is larger, update the current largest.
4. After processing all elements, output the current largest.

Algorithm Design Techniques

Designing algorithms is an art and a science, requiring systematic approaches to problem-solving. Several **algorithm design techniques** help ensure that an algorithm is efficient and correct. Here are some key approaches:

1. Brute Force

Brute force algorithms are the simplest to understand and implement. These algorithms try all possible solutions and are often inefficient. While brute force is not always the best option for large datasets, it is effective when the problem size is small or when no better solution is known.

- **Example**: Checking if a string is a palindrome by reversing it and comparing it to the original string.
- **Complexity**: Brute force algorithms tend to have high time complexity, often $O(n^2)$, $O(n!)$, or worse, depending on the problem.

2. Divide and Conquer

Divide and conquer is a popular technique where a problem is broken down into smaller subproblems, solved independently, and then combined to form the solution to the original problem. This method is highly effective for many types of problems and is particularly useful for large-scale data.

- **Example**: The **Merge Sort** algorithm splits the array into two halves, recursively sorts each half, and then merges them back together.
- **Complexity**: Divide and conquer algorithms often have time complexities like O(n log n), which are much faster than brute force algorithms.

Steps:

1. Divide the problem into subproblems.
2. Solve each subproblem recursively.
3. Combine the results to solve the original problem.

3. Greedy Algorithms

Greedy algorithms make a series of choices by picking the best option available at each step, with the hope of finding the globally optimal solution. Greedy methods are often simpler and faster but may not always yield the best results for all problems.

- **Example**: **Dijkstra's algorithm** for finding the shortest path in a graph uses a greedy approach by choosing the shortest known distance at each step.
- **Complexity**: Greedy algorithms are typically efficient, often with time complexities of $O(n \log n)$ or $O(n)$.

Steps:

1. Choose the best solution at each step.
2. Make decisions based on local optimization.
3. Once a decision is made, move on without revisiting it.

4. Dynamic Programming

Dynamic programming is used to solve problems that can be broken down into overlapping subproblems. Rather than solving each subproblem multiple times, dynamic programming solves each subproblem once and stores the result to avoid redundant computations.

- **Example**: The **Fibonacci sequence** can be efficiently calculated using dynamic programming by storing previously computed values.
- **Complexity**: Dynamic programming often reduces time complexity from exponential ($O(2^n)$) to polynomial ($O(n^2)$ or $O(n)$).

Steps:

1. Break the problem into smaller subproblems.
2. Store the results of subproblems to avoid redundant computation.
3. Combine the subproblem solutions to get the final result.

5. Backtracking

Backtracking is a technique used to find all solutions to a problem by exploring all possible solutions incrementally and backtracking as soon as an invalid solution path is found. It's particularly useful for solving constraint satisfaction problems.

- **Example**: The **N-Queens problem**, where the goal is to place N queens on an N×N chessboard such that no two queens threaten each other, is often solved using backtracking.
- **Complexity**: The time complexity of backtracking algorithms depends on the number of possibilities to be explored.

Steps:

1. Incrementally build the solution.
2. If the current solution path is invalid, backtrack by removing the last step and trying another possibility.
3. Continue until a valid solution is found.

Examples: Searching, Sorting, and Recursion

The following are some classic examples of algorithms:

1. Searching Algorithms

Searching algorithms are used to find a specific element or value within a collection of data (e.g., a list or array).

Linear Search (Brute force approach):

- **Idea**: Start from the first element and check each element until the target is found.
- **Time Complexity**: O(n)
- **Use case**: Suitable for unsorted data.

Binary Search (Divide and conquer approach):

- **Idea**: Given a sorted array, repeatedly divide the array in half and compare the middle element to the target.
- **Time Complexity**: O(log n)
- **Use case**: Efficient for large sorted datasets.

Python Example (Binary Search):

```python
def binary_search(arr, target):
    low, high = 0, len(arr) - 1
    while low <= high:
        mid = (low + high) // 2
        if arr[mid] == target:
            return mid
        elif arr[mid] < target:
            low = mid + 1
        else:
            high = mid - 1
    return -1
```

2. Sorting Algorithms

Sorting algorithms arrange data in a particular order (ascending or descending). There are many sorting algorithms, each with different performance characteristics.

Bubble Sort (Brute force approach):

- **Idea**: Repeatedly step through the list, compare adjacent elements, and swap them if they are in the wrong order.
- **Time Complexity**: $O(n^2)$
- **Use case**: Simple, but inefficient for large datasets.

Quick Sort (Divide and conquer approach):

- **Idea**: Pick a "pivot" element, partition the array around the pivot such that smaller elements go to one side and larger elements to the other, then recursively apply the same process to each side.
- **Time Complexity**: $O(n \log n)$ on average.
- **Use case**: Fast for large datasets.

Python Example (Quick Sort):

```
def quicksort(arr):

    if len(arr) <= 1:

        return arr

    pivot = arr[len(arr) // 2]

    left = [x for x in arr if x < pivot]

    middle = [x for x in arr if x == pivot]

    right = [x for x in arr if x > pivot]

    return quicksort(left) + middle +
quicksort(right)
```

3. Recursion

Recursion is the process where a function calls itself to solve a smaller instance of the same problem. Recursive algorithms are often simpler to understand and implement, especially for problems that involve repetitive tasks or hierarchical structures.

Example: Factorial Function:

- **Idea**: The factorial of a number n is the product of all integers from 1 to n. The factorial function can be defined recursively as:
factorial(n)=n×factorial(n−1) for n>1\text{factorial}(n) = n \times \text{factorial}(n-1) \text{ for } n > 1
factorial(1)=1\text{factorial}(1) = 1

Python Example (Factorial Function):

```
def factorial(n):

    if n == 1:

        return 1

    else:

        return n * factorial(n - 1)
```

Summary

Algorithms are essential tools for problem-solving and optimizing computational tasks. Understanding the principles of algorithm design can help developers create more efficient programs. Key points from this section include:

1. **What is an Algorithm?**: A sequence of well-defined steps to solve a problem.
2. **Algorithm Design Techniques**: Brute force, divide and conquer, greedy algorithms, dynamic programming, and backtracking.
3. **Examples**:
    - ○ **Searching**: Linear search and binary search.
    - ○ **Sorting**: Bubble sort, quick sort, and other sorting algorithms.
    - ○ **Recursion**: Solving problems by calling a function within itself.

Basics of Databases

Databases are critical to modern applications and systems, serving as organized collections of data that can be easily stored, retrieved, and manipulated. Whether you're building a website, mobile application, or enterprise software, understanding databases is essential for managing and utilizing data effectively. This section introduces the basics of databases, including key concepts, database management systems (DBMS), the structure of databases, and how to interact with them using SQL (Structured Query Language).

Introduction to Databases

What is a Database?

A **database** is an organized collection of data that is stored electronically in a computer system. Databases enable users and programs to access, manipulate, and store data efficiently. Unlike traditional file storage, databases allow data to be stored in a structured format, making it easier to query, update, and manage.

- **Structured Data**: Data in a database is typically organized into tables, rows, and columns, making it easy to relate and query the data.
- **Unstructured Data**: Some databases, especially NoSQL databases, support the storage of unstructured data, such as documents, images, and videos.

Database Management Systems (DBMS)

A **Database Management System (DBMS)** is software that interacts with users, applications, and the database itself to manage the data. The DBMS is responsible for storing, retrieving, and managing data in a database. It provides an interface for creating, updating, and querying data. DBMSs can be categorized into two primary types:

1. **Relational DBMS (RDBMS)**: These systems use tables to store data, with relationships between tables defined by keys. They use SQL for querying and managing data.
   - Examples: **MySQL, PostgreSQL, SQLite, Oracle Database**.
2. **NoSQL DBMS**: These systems are designed for unstructured or semi-structured data and often offer more flexibility than relational databases. They are often used in applications requiring scalability and flexibility.
   - Examples: **MongoDB, Cassandra, CouchDB**.

Components of a Database

Databases generally consist of several components:

- **Tables**: The primary structure that holds the data in rows and columns.
- **Rows**: Individual records in a table, each representing a data entry.
- **Columns**: Fields in a table that define the type of data stored in each record.
- **Primary Key**: A unique identifier for each row in a table.
- **Foreign Key**: A key used to establish a relationship between two tables.

Example: Consider a "Customers" table in a relational database:

CustomerID	FirstName	LastName	Email

1	John	Doe	john.doe @email.c om
2	Jane	Smith	jane.smit h@email. com

Here, CustomerID is the primary key, ensuring that each record is uniquely identifiable.

SQL Basics: Queries and CRUD Operations

SQL (Structured Query Language) is the standard language used for interacting with relational databases. It allows users to perform various operations like creating tables, inserting data, retrieving information, updating records, and deleting data.

SQL Queries

SQL queries are commands used to interact with a database. A basic query typically involves selecting, inserting, updating, or deleting data from a database table.

1. SELECT Query (Retrieving Data)

The SELECT statement is used to query a database and retrieve data. You can specify which columns to return and filter results using conditions.

Basic Syntax:

SELECT column1, column2, ...

FROM table_name;

Example: Retrieve all customers from the "Customers" table:

SELECT * FROM Customers;

You can also filter the results with WHERE conditions:

SELECT FirstName, LastName FROM Customers

WHERE LastName = 'Doe';

2. INSERT Query (Inserting Data)

The INSERT INTO statement is used to add new rows of data to a table.

Basic Syntax:

INSERT INTO table_name (column1, column2, ...)

VALUES (value1, value2, ...);

Example: Add a new customer to the "Customers" table:

INSERT INTO Customers (CustomerID, FirstName, LastName, Email)

VALUES (3, 'Alice', 'Johnson', 'alice.johnson@email.com');

3. UPDATE Query (Modifying Data)

The UPDATE statement is used to modify existing records in a table. You can update one or more columns based on specific conditions.

Basic Syntax:

UPDATE table_name

SET column1 = value1, column2 = value2, ...

WHERE condition;

Example: Change the email address of a customer:

UPDATE Customers

SET Email = 'newemail@email.com'

WHERE CustomerID = 1;

4. DELETE Query (Removing Data)

The DELETE statement is used to delete rows from a table. It's important to be careful when using DELETE, as it removes data permanently.

Basic Syntax:

DELETE FROM table_name

WHERE condition;

Example: Delete a customer from the "Customers" table:

DELETE FROM Customers

WHERE CustomerID = 2;

5. Other SQL Clauses and Operations

- **WHERE**: Filters data based on conditions.
- **ORDER BY**: Sorts the results based on one or more columns.
- **GROUP BY**: Groups rows sharing a property, often used with aggregate functions (e.g., COUNT(), AVG()).
- **JOIN**: Combines data from two or more tables based on a related column.

Example (Using JOIN): Retrieve customer orders from two related tables ("Customers" and "Orders"):

SELECT Customers.FirstName, Customers.LastName, Orders.OrderID

FROM Customers

JOIN Orders ON Customers.CustomerID = Orders.CustomerID;

Integrating Databases with Code

Interacting with databases from code is a common task for many types of applications. Most programming languages provide libraries or frameworks for interacting with relational databases and performing SQL queries.

1. Using SQL with Python

Python provides several libraries for database interaction, including **sqlite3** (for SQLite databases), **PyMySQL**, and **psycopg2** (for MySQL and PostgreSQL databases). Below is an example using the sqlite3 library to connect to a SQLite database and perform basic SQL operations.

Example (Connecting to SQLite and performing CRUD operations):

```
import sqlite3
```

```python
# Connect to the database (or create it if it
doesn't exist)

conn = sqlite3.connect('example.db')

cursor = conn.cursor()


# Create a table

cursor.execute('''CREATE TABLE IF NOT
EXISTS Customers

        (CustomerID INTEGER PRIMARY
KEY, FirstName TEXT, LastName TEXT, Email
TEXT)''')


# Insert a record

cursor.execute('''INSERT INTO Customers
(CustomerID, FirstName, LastName, Email)

        VALUES (1, 'John', 'Doe',
'john.doe@email.com')''')
```

```python
# Retrieve data

cursor.execute('SELECT * FROM Customers')

print(cursor.fetchall())  # Output: [(1, 'John',
'Doe', 'john.doe@email.com')]


# Update data

cursor.execute('UPDATE Customers SET Email
= "new.email@email.com" WHERE
CustomerID = 1')


# Delete data

cursor.execute('DELETE FROM Customers
WHERE CustomerID = 1')


# Commit changes and close the connection
```

conn.commit()

conn.close()

2. Using SQL with Java

Java interacts with databases through the **JDBC (Java Database Connectivity)** API, which allows applications to execute SQL queries against a database.

Example (Connecting to MySQL and performing CRUD operations):

```java
import java.sql.*;


public class DatabaseExample {

    public static void main(String[] args) {

        try {

            // Connect to the database
```

```
        Connection conn =
DriverManager.getConnection("jdbc:mysql://loc
alhost:3306/testdb", "root", "password");

        Statement stmt = conn.createStatement();


        // Create a table

        String createTableSQL = "CREATE
TABLE IF NOT EXISTS Customers
(CustomerID INT PRIMARY KEY, FirstName
VARCHAR(50), LastName VARCHAR(50),
Email VARCHAR(100))";

        stmt.executeUpdate(createTableSQL);


        // Insert a record

        String insertSQL = "INSERT INTO
Customers (CustomerID, FirstName, LastName,
Email) VALUES (1, 'John', 'Doe',
'john.doe@email.com')";
```

```
stmt.executeUpdate(insertSQL);


// Retrieve data

ResultSet rs =
stmt.executeQuery("SELECT * FROM
Customers");

while (rs.next()) {


System.out.println(rs.getInt("CustomerID") + ",
" + rs.getString("FirstName") + ", " +
rs.getString("LastName") + ", " +
rs.getString("Email"));

}


// Update data

String updateSQL = "UPDATE
Customers SET Email = 'new.email@email.com'
WHERE CustomerID = 1";
```

```
stmt.executeUpdate(updateSQL);


// Delete data

String deleteSQL = "DELETE FROM
Customers WHERE CustomerID = 1";

stmt.executeUpdate(deleteSQL);


// Close the connection

conn.close();
} catch (SQLException e) {

e.printStackTrace();

}

}

}
```

3. Using SQL with Node.js

Node.js can interact with databases using libraries like **node-postgres** (for PostgreSQL) or **mysql2** (for MySQL). Below is an

example using the mysql2 library to connect to a MySQL database.

Example (Connecting to MySQL with Node.js):

```
const mysql = require('mysql2');
```

```
// Create a connection to the database
const connection = mysql.createConnection({
  host: 'localhost',
  user: 'root',
  password: 'password',
  database: 'testdb'
```

```
});
```

```
// Create a table

connection.query('CREATE TABLE IF NOT
EXISTS Customers (CustomerID INT
PRIMARY KEY, FirstName VARCHAR(50),
LastName VARCHAR(50), Email
VARCHAR(100))', (err, results) => {

  if (err) throw err;

  console.log('Table created');

});
```

```
// Insert a record

connection.query('INSERT INTO Customers
(CustomerID, FirstName, LastName, Email)
VALUES (1, "John", "Doe",
"john.doe@email.com")', (err, results) => {

  if (err) throw err;
```

```
  console.log('Record inserted');

});


// Retrieve data

connection.query('SELECT * FROM
Customers', (err, results) => {

  if (err) throw err;

  console.log(results);

});


// Close the connection

connection.end();
```

Summary

1. **What is a Database?** A database is an organized collection of data that can be efficiently managed, stored, and retrieved using a DBMS.

2. **SQL Basics**: SQL is the language used to interact with relational databases. Key operations include:
   - SELECT: Retrieve data.
   - INSERT: Add new records.
   - UPDATE: Modify existing records.
   - DELETE: Remove records.

3. **Integrating Databases with Code**: Programming languages like Python, Java, and JavaScript provide libraries or APIs to interact with databases, enabling developers to integrate database operations into their applications.

Introduction to Web Programming

Web programming is an essential skill for developers looking to build interactive, dynamic, and user-friendly applications accessible via the internet. Whether you're building a simple static webpage or a complex dynamic web application, web programming forms the backbone of modern web development. This section covers the basics of web programming, including the fundamentals of HTTP, APIs, and the distinction between front-end and back-end programming. Additionally, we will walk through the steps of building a simple web application.

Basics of HTTP and APIs

What is HTTP?

HTTP (HyperText Transfer Protocol) is the foundational protocol used by the World Wide Web. It defines the rules and conventions for how clients (typically web browsers) and servers communicate with each other. When a user types a URL in their browser, the browser sends an HTTP request to the server hosting the website, which then responds with the appropriate content.

Key Components of HTTP:

1. **Request and Response**: HTTP follows a request-response model. The client sends an HTTP request, and the server responds with an HTTP response.
2. **Methods**: HTTP methods define the action to be performed on the server:
   - **GET**: Retrieve data from the server.
   - **POST**: Send data to the server (e.g., form submissions).

- ○ **PUT**: Update data on the server.
- ○ **DELETE**: Remove data from the server.
3. **Status Codes**: HTTP responses come with a status code, which indicates the result of the request:
   - ○ **200 OK**: Request was successful.
   - ○ **404 Not Found**: The requested resource does not exist.
   - ○ **500 Internal Server Error**: A server-side error occurred.

Example of an HTTP Request: When you visit http://example.com, the browser sends a **GET** request to the server:

GET / HTTP/1.1

Host: example.com

User-Agent: Mozilla/5.0 ...

Accept:
text/html,application/xhtml+xml,application/xml
;q=0.9,image/webp,*/*;q=0.8

The server might respond with:

HTTP/1.1 200 OK

Content-Type: text/html; charset=UTF-8

Date: Mon, 01 Jan 2025 12:00:00 GMT

Content-Length: 1245

What is an API?

An **API (Application Programming Interface)** is a set of rules and protocols that allow different software applications to communicate with each other. Web APIs allow applications to interact over the web, typically using HTTP requests. APIs can be public (allowing third-party access) or private (used internally within a system).

APIs are commonly used for tasks like:

- **Fetching data**: Web APIs allow you to retrieve information from a server or database, such as pulling data from a weather service or social media platform.

- **Interacting with external services**: Many applications interact with external services like payment gateways (Stripe, PayPal) or social media APIs (Twitter, Facebook).

RESTful APIs:

- **REST (Representational State Transfer)** is a popular architectural style for designing APIs, which uses HTTP methods (GET, POST, PUT, DELETE) to operate on resources (objects or data) represented as URLs.
- **JSON (JavaScript Object Notation)** is the most common format for sending data between a client and a server in a RESTful API.

Example of a RESTful API Request: Suppose you want to get the weather information for a city using a weather API:

GET
/weather?city=London&appid=YOUR_API_KE
Y HTTP/1.1

Host: api.weather.com

The server might respond with a JSON object
containing the weather data:

```
{

  "city": "London",

  "temperature": 15,

  "description": "Cloudy",

  "humidity": 80

}
```


APIs simplify integrating external functionality
into your web application, such as adding user

authentication, sending emails, or retrieving product information.

Front-End vs. Back-End Programming

Web development is typically divided into two main parts: **front-end** and **back-end** programming. These two areas work together to create a fully functional web application, each handling different tasks.

Front-End Programming

Front-end programming refers to the development of the user interface (UI) and user experience (UX) aspects of a website or application. It involves everything that the user interacts with directly in their web browser.

- **Languages**: Front-end development primarily uses:
  - **HTML (Hypertext Markup Language)**: The structural foundation of webpages, used to

create elements like headings, paragraphs, links, forms, and images.

- ○ **CSS (Cascading Style Sheets)**: Used to style and layout HTML elements, controlling the design, colors, fonts, and overall appearance.
- ○ **JavaScript**: A programming language that enables dynamic and interactive elements on webpages, such as animations, form validation, and content updates without refreshing the page.

Key Front-End Concepts:

- **Responsive Design**: Ensuring a website is usable on various devices (desktops, tablets, smartphones) by using fluid grids, media queries, and flexible images.
- **DOM (Document Object Model)**: A tree-like representation of the HTML structure. JavaScript interacts with the

DOM to dynamically change webpage content.

- **AJAX (Asynchronous JavaScript and XML)**: A technique used to make asynchronous requests to the server (e.g., loading new data) without reloading the entire page.

Front-End Frameworks and Libraries:

- **React**: A JavaScript library for building user interfaces, particularly for single-page applications (SPAs).
- **Vue.js**: A progressive JavaScript framework for building interactive UIs and SPAs.
- **Angular**: A full-fledged front-end framework for building dynamic and complex web applications.

Back-End Programming

Back-end programming refers to the server-side part of web development. It handles the logic, database interactions, authentication, and overall application functionality that the user does not see.

- **Languages**: Back-end development typically involves languages like:
  - ○ **Python**: A versatile language used for web development with frameworks like **Django** and **Flask**.
  - ○ **Java**: A powerful language used for building large-scale web applications, with frameworks like **Spring**.
  - ○ **Ruby**: Often used with the **Ruby on Rails** framework for building web applications quickly.
  - ○ **PHP**: A widely-used language for web development, particularly in content management systems like **WordPress**.
  - ○ **Node.js**: A JavaScript runtime that allows developers to build server-side applications using JavaScript.

Key Back-End Concepts:

- **Databases**: Back-end developers interact with databases (e.g., MySQL, PostgreSQL, MongoDB) to store and retrieve data for the application.
- **Authentication and Authorization**: Back-end programming includes managing user authentication (logging in) and authorization (determining what a user can access).
- **APIs**: Back-end developers often design and maintain APIs to allow front-end applications to interact with the server and retrieve or send data.
- **Server Management**: Back-end developers manage servers and deployment, ensuring the application runs smoothly and efficiently.

Back-End Frameworks:

- **Express.js** (Node.js): A minimalist framework for building server-side applications with JavaScript.
- **Django** (Python): A high-level framework for rapid web application development

with built-in features like authentication, URL routing, and database management.

- **Ruby on Rails**: A full-stack framework that emphasizes convention over configuration, enabling fast development of web applications.

Building a Simple Web Application

Now that we understand the basic concepts of web programming, let's walk through the steps to build a simple web application that incorporates both front-end and back-end components. In this example, we'll build a basic **To-Do list app** where users can add, view, and delete tasks.

Step 1: Set Up the Front-End

We will create a simple HTML page for the UI of our To-Do list. It will contain an input field to add new tasks and a list to display tasks.

HTML (index.html):

```
<!DOCTYPE html>

<html lang="en">

<head>

  <meta charset="UTF-8">

  <meta name="viewport"
content="width=device-width,
initial-scale=1.0">

  <title>To-Do List</title>

  <link rel="stylesheet" href="style.css">

</head>

<body>

  <div class="todo-container">

    <h1>My To-Do List</h1>

    <input type="text" id="taskInput"
placeholder="Add a new task...">
```

```
    <button onclick="addTask()">Add
Task</button>

    <ul id="taskList"></ul>

  </div>

  <script src="script.js"></script>

</body>

</html>
```

CSS (style.css):

```css
body {

    font-family: Arial, sans-serif;

    text-align: center;

    margin-top: 50px;

}
```

```
.todo-container {

   max-width: 400px;

   margin: 0 auto;

}


input {

   padding: 10px;

   width: 300px;

}


button {

   padding: 10px;

   background-color: #4CAF50;

   color: white;

   border: none;
```

```
    cursor: pointer;

}


ul {

    list-style-type: none;

    padding: 0;

}


li {

    padding: 10px;

    margin: 5px;

    background-color: #f9f
```

Version Control Systems (VCS)

Version control is a fundamental aspect of modern software development, providing a way to manage and track changes to code over time. It allows developers to work on projects simultaneously without losing their progress or introducing errors.

What is Version Control?

Version control is a system that allows multiple developers (or even a single developer) to track, manage, and manage changes to source code over time. It keeps a history of changes made to a project, allowing developers to revert to previous versions of code, compare changes, and manage multiple versions of the codebase simultaneously.

Why Use Version Control?

1. **Track Changes**: Every time code is updated, version control records the changes, including the who, what, and when of those changes. This makes it easy to see how the project evolves over time and who contributed what.

2. **Collaboration**: Multiple developers can work on the same project without overwriting each other's work. Version control systems help merge contributions and resolve conflicts in code.

3. **Revert to Previous Versions**: If a change introduces a bug or breaks functionality, version control allows you to revert to a previous version where everything was working as expected.

4. **Branching and Merging**: Developers can work on new features or fixes in isolation

(branches) and later merge them back into the main project without affecting the main codebase.

5. **Backup and Restore**: In case of data loss or system failure, version control acts as a backup, enabling you to restore the project to a previous state.

Git Basics: Repositories, Commits, and Branching

Git is a **distributed version control system** that allows developers to work independently on a local copy of the code and later synchronize with a remote repository. It is the most widely-used version control system today, powering platforms like GitHub, GitLab, and Bitbucket.

Repositories (Repos)

A **repository** is a collection of files and directories where your project lives. It contains all of your project's files and the complete version history. A repository can be:

- **Local**: The version-controlled project stored on your local computer.
- **Remote**: A repository hosted on a server (e.g., GitHub, GitLab, or Bitbucket) where developers can push and pull changes.

You initialize a Git repository in your project's directory using the following command:

git init

This command creates a .git directory in your project folder, where Git stores its version history.

Commits

A **commit** is a snapshot of the changes made to the project. Every time you make a change to the code, you "commit" it, which means you are saving a snapshot of those changes with a descriptive message.

Each commit has:

- **A unique identifier** (commit hash) generated by Git.
- **A commit message** describing the changes made.
- **Author information** (who made the change).
- **A timestamp** indicating when the commit was made.

To commit changes:

1. First, you stage the changes with git add (which selects the files you want to include in the commit).
2. Then, you create the commit with git commit.

Example:

git add index.html

git commit -m "Updated the homepage layout"

A commit creates a checkpoint, so you can later review or revert to any previous commit in the project's history.

Branching

Branching is a powerful feature of Git, allowing you to work on multiple versions of a project simultaneously. When you create a branch, you diverge from the main codebase (usually called master or main) and can work on new features, bug fixes, or experiments in isolation.

- **Main branch**: The default branch where the stable version of the project lives.
- **Feature branch**: A branch created to work on a new feature or fix.
- **Merge**: Once you finish working on a branch, you can merge it back into the main branch.

To create a new branch:

git branch feature-xyz

To switch between branches:

git checkout feature-xyz

Once the work is complete, you merge the branch back into the main branch:

git checkout main

git merge feature-xyz

Branching is crucial when multiple developers work on different aspects of a project simultaneously without interfering with each other's work.

Basic Git Workflow

Here's a simple sequence of Git commands you'll use regularly:

1. git init - Initialize a new repository.
2. git status - Check the current status of your repository.

3. git add <file> - Stage a file to be committed.
4. git commit -m "message" - Commit staged files with a descriptive message.
5. git push - Push your local commits to a remote repository (e.g., GitHub).
6. git pull - Fetch and merge changes from a remote repository into your local repository.
7. git clone <repo_url> - Clone a remote repository to your local machine.

Collaborating on Code

One of the most important features of version control is the ability to collaborate on code with other developers, whether they are across the room or across the world. Git facilitates smooth collaboration through various tools and workflows.

Cloning a Repository

To work on an existing project, you clone the remote repository onto your local machine:

git clone
https://github.com/username/repository.git

This command downloads the entire project history, allowing you to start working on it locally.

Pulling Changes

When collaborating on a team project, it's essential to stay up-to-date with the latest changes. You can fetch the latest changes from the remote repository using:

git pull

This command fetches the changes made by others and merges them into your local branch.

Resolving Merge Conflicts

When working in teams, merge conflicts can
arise. A **merge conflict** occurs when two
developers modify the same part of the same file
differently, and Git cannot automatically
reconcile the differences.

For example, if two developers change the same
line of code, Git will highlight the conflict, and it
will be up to the developer to manually resolve
the conflict.

Example conflict in a file:

<<<<<<< HEAD

This is my version of the code.

=======

This is your version of the code.

>>>>>>> feature-xyz

In this case, the developer must choose which version to keep (or combine them) and then commit the resolved changes.

Pull Requests (PRs) / Merge Requests (MRs)

Once you've completed your work on a feature or bug fix in a branch, you can submit it for review using a **pull request** (GitHub) or **merge request** (GitLab). A pull request is a request to merge your changes into the main project branch (e.g., main or master).

- The pull request includes the changes you made and allows other team members to review and discuss those changes before merging them into the main codebase.
- This process encourages code review, where teammates inspect your code for bugs, functionality, and readability before the changes are integrated.

Forking

Forking is another collaboration feature that allows you to copy an entire repository to your own GitHub account. Forks are useful when contributing to open-source projects or working on an external project without affecting the original repository.

Once you fork a project, you can clone it to your local machine, make changes, and submit pull requests to the original repository.

Git Hosting Platforms

Platforms like **GitHub**, **GitLab**, and **Bitbucket** provide hosting services for Git repositories, making it easier for teams to collaborate on code. These platforms also offer additional features such as:

- **Issue tracking**: Allows you to track bugs, tasks, and feature requests.
- **Continuous Integration/Continuous Deployment (CI/CD)**: Automates the process of testing, building, and deploying code.

- **Wikis and documentation**: Provide spaces to maintain documentation for the project.

Summary

- **Version Control** is essential for managing changes in code, tracking project history, and enabling collaboration between developers.
- **Git** is the most widely-used version control system, and it includes powerful features like **commits**, **branching**, and **merging**.
- Collaboration is made easy with features such as **cloning repositories**, **pulling changes**, and **pull requests**.
- Git hosting platforms like **GitHub** and **GitLab** enhance collaboration by providing additional tools for issue tracking, documentation, and CI/CD.

Testing and Quality Assurance

Testing and quality assurance (QA) are essential aspects of the software development process. They ensure that the application is functioning as expected, meeting the user's requirements, and maintaining a high standard of quality. The goal of testing is not only to identify bugs and issues but also to verify that the software performs well under different conditions and is of a high enough quality to be deployed in production.

Unit Testing and Test-Driven Development (TDD)

What is Unit Testing?

Unit testing involves testing individual components or units of a program in isolation. A unit is typically a small part of the code, such as a single function or method. The main purpose of unit testing is to validate that each unit performs as expected, in isolation, without relying on external components or dependencies.

In unit testing, you write test cases that define the expected behavior of a unit. These tests run automatically, providing a way to catch bugs early in the development process.

Benefits of Unit Testing:

- **Early bug detection**: Unit tests catch issues at the very beginning of the development process, which can prevent more significant problems from occurring later on.

- **Improved code design**: Writing unit tests encourages developers to break down complex logic into smaller, more manageable functions, leading to cleaner, more modular code.
- **Simplifies refactoring**: Unit tests provide a safety net when making changes or refactoring code, ensuring that changes don't unintentionally break existing functionality.
- **Automated regression testing**: Unit tests can be rerun every time the code changes to ensure that no new bugs have been introduced.

Example of Unit Testing in JavaScript (using Jest):

Let's say you have a simple function add(a, b) that adds two numbers together.

```
function add(a, b) {
```

```
    return a + b;

}
```

You can write a unit test using a framework like Jest to ensure this function works as expected:

```
const add = require('./add');
```

```
test('adds two numbers correctly', () => {

  expect(add(1, 2)).toBe(3);

  expect(add(-1, 1)).toBe(0);

  expect(add(0, 0)).toBe(0);

});
```

This test checks that the add function correctly sums various pairs of numbers. Running this test will ensure that the add function behaves as expected.

What is Test-Driven Development (TDD)?

Test-Driven Development (TDD) is a software development methodology where tests are written before the actual code. In TDD, developers follow a strict cycle of writing tests, writing code to pass the tests, and then refactoring the code to improve it while ensuring the tests still pass.

The TDD cycle is often referred to as **Red-Green-Refactor**:

1. **Red**: Write a failing test that defines the functionality you want to implement.
2. **Green**: Write just enough code to make the test pass.
3. **Refactor**: Improve the code while ensuring that the test still passes.

Benefits of TDD:

- **Better test coverage**: Writing tests first helps ensure all parts of the code are tested.
- **Fewer bugs**: By testing code from the outset, developers catch issues early.
- **Refactoring with confidence**: TDD ensures that refactored code maintains the same functionality.

Example of TDD in JavaScript:

Let's apply TDD to create a function multiply(a, b) that multiplies two numbers.

Red: Write a failing test:

```
test('multiplies two numbers', () => {

  expect(multiply(2, 3)).toBe(6);

});
```

Green: Write just enough code to pass the test:

```
function multiply(a, b) {
```

```
return a * b;

}
```

Refactor: Refactor the function (if necessary), ensuring it still passes the test:

```
function multiply(a, b) {

return a * b;

}
```

By following the TDD cycle, we ensure that the function is both tested and functioning correctly from the start.

Integration and System Testing

What is Integration Testing?

Integration testing is the process of testing the interactions between different modules or components of a system. It verifies that individual components, which have already been tested through unit tests, work together as expected. Integration testing is typically performed after unit testing and focuses on the interfaces between components.

For example, if you have a User module that handles user data and a Database module that interacts with a database, integration testing will ensure that data flows correctly from the User module to the Database and vice versa.

Types of Integration Testing:

- **Big Bang Integration Testing**: All components are integrated at once, and the system is tested as a whole.
- **Incremental Integration Testing**: Components are integrated one at a time, and each is tested as it is added.

What is System Testing?

System testing involves testing the entire system as a whole. This type of testing evaluates the functionality, performance, and stability of the system as a whole in a controlled environment, ensuring that all integrated components function correctly together.

System testing includes:

- **Functional testing**: Verifying that the system meets the specified functional requirements.
- **Non-functional testing**: Testing aspects such as performance, security, and usability.
- **End-to-End testing**: Ensuring the entire system, including external dependencies and integrations, functions as expected.

Example of system testing might include validating a web application by simulating real-world user interactions, such as creating an account, logging in, and performing various tasks, to ensure everything works as intended.

Code Reviews and Best Practices

What is a Code Review?

A **code review** is a process where one or more developers examine another developer's code to ensure it meets coding standards, is free of bugs, and adheres to best practices. Code reviews are an essential part of ensuring code quality, improving collaboration among team members, and spreading knowledge within the team.

Benefits of Code Reviews:

- **Improved code quality**: Reviewers catch mistakes, bugs, and design issues that the original developer may have missed.
- **Knowledge sharing**: Code reviews allow team members to learn from each other, improving skills and consistency across the team.
- **Consistency**: Ensures that all code adheres to the team's coding standards, resulting in a more readable and maintainable codebase.

Best Practices for Code Reviews:

1. **Be respectful and constructive**: Provide feedback that is helpful and focused on the code, not the developer.
2. **Focus on key issues**: Prioritize the review of bugs, readability, maintainability, and security concerns.
3. **Keep it small**: Review small, incremental changes rather than large code dumps to make the review process more manageable.
4. **Use tools**: Utilize code review tools such as GitHub Pull Requests, GitLab Merge Requests, or Bitbucket's Pull Requests to streamline the review process.
5. **Ensure tests are in place**: Make sure the code is well-tested before submitting it for review.

Best Practices for Writing Testable Code:

- **Modular design**: Write functions or methods that are small and focused on one task, making them easier to test.

- **Avoid side effects**: Keep functions pure (i.e., no external state changes) to ensure predictable behavior.
- **Write meaningful tests**: Test both typical and edge cases to ensure comprehensive test coverage.
- **Document tests**: Write clear, descriptive test names and comments explaining what the test is doing.

Summary

1. **Unit Testing** is essential for verifying the correctness of individual components in isolation, helping catch bugs early and improving code quality.
2. **Test-Driven Development (TDD)** encourages writing tests before code, ensuring that the software meets requirements from the start and improving code design.
3. **Integration Testing** ensures that different modules of a system interact as expected,

while **System Testing** tests the entire
system for correctness and performance.

4. **Code Reviews** promote collaboration,
   knowledge sharing, and code quality,
   ensuring that the final product is
   maintainable, secure, and efficient.

Introduction to Software Development Methodologies

In software development, methodologies provide structured approaches and frameworks that guide the development process. Choosing the right software development methodology is crucial for the success of a project, as it affects the project's planning, execution, communication, and eventual delivery. In this section, we will explore popular software development methodologies such as Waterfall, Agile, and DevOps, the Software Development Lifecycle (SDLC), and the importance of collaboration tools and practices in ensuring a smooth development process.

Waterfall vs. Agile vs. DevOps

Waterfall Methodology

The **Waterfall** methodology is one of the earliest and most traditional approaches to software development. It is a linear and sequential approach where the entire software development process is divided into distinct phases, and each phase must be completed before moving on to the next. These phases typically include:

1. **Requirements Gathering**: The project requirements are thoroughly gathered and documented.
2. **System Design**: The architecture and design of the software are planned.
3. **Implementation**: The software is developed according to the design specifications.

4. **Testing**: The system is tested to ensure it meets the required specifications and is free of bugs.
5. **Deployment**: The software is deployed to the users or the production environment.
6. **Maintenance**: The system undergoes updates, bug fixes, and improvements as needed.

Advantages of Waterfall:

- **Clear structure**: The clear separation of phases makes it easy to understand the project lifecycle.
- **Easy to manage**: With well-defined deliverables for each phase, it's relatively easy to track progress.
- **Stable requirements**: Waterfall is most suitable for projects with stable and well-understood requirements that are unlikely to change.

Disadvantages of Waterfall:

- **Inflexibility**: Once a phase is completed, it is difficult to go back and make changes, making it less flexible for handling evolving requirements.
- **Late testing**: Testing occurs only after the development phase is completed, so bugs and issues may be harder to fix and more costly to resolve.
- **Long delivery time**: Since the project must go through each phase sequentially, it can take a long time to deliver the final product.

Waterfall is typically suited for projects where the requirements are clearly defined at the start, and there is little room for change throughout the process, such as regulatory or compliance-based projects.

Agile Methodology

Agile is an iterative and flexible software development methodology that emphasizes collaboration, adaptability, and customer feedback. Unlike Waterfall, Agile focuses on delivering small, functional pieces of software in short development cycles, called **iterations** or **sprints**. Agile methodologies include frameworks such as **Scrum**, **Kanban**, and **Extreme Programming (XP)**.

The key principles of Agile are:

1. **Customer collaboration over contract negotiation**: Agile emphasizes constant interaction with the customer or product owner to ensure the software meets their needs.
2. **Responding to change over following a plan**: Agile welcomes changes in requirements, even late in the development process.
3. **Delivering working software frequently**: Agile encourages delivering functional software at regular intervals, typically every 2-4 weeks, to allow for quicker feedback and adjustments.
4. **Cross-functional teams**: Agile teams are typically made up of developers, testers,

designers, and product owners who collaborate closely throughout the project.

Advantages of Agile:

- **Flexibility**: Agile is highly adaptable and allows changes to be made at any point in the project, making it suitable for dynamic projects with evolving requirements.
- **Frequent delivery**: The iterative approach results in frequent releases of working software, which allows stakeholders to see progress early and often.
- **Improved collaboration**: Regular communication and feedback from stakeholders and team members help ensure that the product aligns with customer needs.
- **Higher quality**: Continuous testing and integration help ensure higher-quality software and faster identification of defects.

Disadvantages of Agile:

- **Unclear end goal**: With evolving requirements and frequent changes, it can be challenging to define the scope and deliverables clearly at the start of the project.
- **Time and resource-intensive**: Agile requires continuous involvement from stakeholders and team members, which can be demanding in terms of time and resources.
- **Difficult to scale**: While Agile works well for small to medium-sized projects, scaling it across large teams and complex projects can become challenging.

Agile is ideal for projects that require flexibility, innovation, and frequent updates, such as web applications, startups, or projects with rapidly changing requirements.

DevOps Methodology

DevOps is a methodology that emphasizes the collaboration between development and operations teams to automate and streamline the process of software development, testing, deployment, and maintenance. The goal of DevOps is to shorten the development lifecycle and ensure that software can be delivered reliably and at high velocity. DevOps combines aspects of **Agile** with **continuous integration** and **continuous delivery** (CI/CD), infrastructure as code, and automated monitoring.

Key principles of DevOps include:

1. **Automation**: Automating the software delivery process, including testing, integration, and deployment, to reduce manual intervention and improve speed.
2. **Collaboration**: Encouraging collaboration between developers, operations, and other stakeholders to break down silos and improve communication.
3. **Continuous Integration and Continuous Delivery (CI/CD)**: Ensuring that new code is integrated frequently and deployed automatically, with automated testing to ensure quality at each step.

4. **Monitoring and Feedback**: Continuous monitoring of the software in production to identify performance issues, bugs, and opportunities for improvement.

Advantages of DevOps:

- **Faster delivery**: Automation of the development and deployment process allows for faster releases and frequent updates.
- **Improved collaboration**: By bringing together development and operations teams, DevOps fosters a culture of collaboration and shared responsibility.
- **High-quality software**: Automated testing, monitoring, and feedback loops ensure that software is consistently of high quality and performs well in production.
- **Scalability**: DevOps practices, such as containerization and cloud infrastructure, enable scalable solutions that can adapt to growing demands.

Disadvantages of DevOps:

- **Cultural shift**: DevOps requires a significant cultural change within an organization, which can be difficult to implement and sustain.
- **Initial setup**: Setting up automation, CI/CD pipelines, and integrated monitoring systems can be time-consuming and complex.
- **Learning curve**: Developers and operations teams may need to learn new tools and practices to effectively implement DevOps.

DevOps is particularly suited for projects that require continuous integration, fast releases, and frequent updates, such as cloud-based applications, e-commerce platforms, and software as a service (SaaS) products.

Understanding the Software Development Lifecycle (SDLC)

The **Software Development Lifecycle (SDLC)**
is a structured approach to software development
that defines the stages involved in building
software from initial concept to deployment and
maintenance. The SDLC outlines a series of
well-defined phases that are typically followed
in both Waterfall and Agile methodologies,
though their implementation can vary. The
standard SDLC phases include:

1. **Planning**: In this phase, the project scope,
   goals, resources, and timelines are
   defined. Planning also includes risk
   analysis and identifying key stakeholders.
2. **Feasibility Study**: Analyzing the project's
   feasibility in terms of technology, cost,
   time, and resources.
3. **System Design**: Defining the architecture,
   components, and technical specifications
   required for the system. This phase often
   includes creating prototypes and
   wireframes.
4. **Development**: Writing the actual code for
   the system. This phase involves

translating design documents into executable software.

5. **Testing**: The system undergoes rigorous testing to ensure that it meets the requirements and is free of defects. Testing can include unit tests, integration tests, system tests, and user acceptance tests.

6. **Deployment**: The system is deployed to a production environment for end users to access. This phase includes preparing deployment scripts and ensuring that the system can be smoothly installed and configured.

7. **Maintenance**: After deployment, the system enters a phase of ongoing maintenance, where bug fixes, updates, and new features are implemented based on user feedback and evolving requirements.

The SDLC ensures that each phase of the software development process is well-organized and well-documented, leading to the efficient production of high-quality software.

Collaboration Tools and Practices

Collaboration is a crucial component of modern software development, especially for distributed teams. Various tools and practices are used to facilitate communication, manage tasks, track progress, and ensure that the team is aligned with the project goals. Some of the most commonly used collaboration tools and practices include:

- **Project Management Tools**: Tools like **Jira, Trello, Asana**, and **Monday.com** help track tasks, sprints, and project milestones. They enable teams to break down large projects into smaller, manageable tasks and track progress over time.
- **Version Control**: Platforms like **GitHub, GitLab**, and **Bitbucket** allow developers

to collaborate on code, track changes, and manage code repositories.

- **Communication Tools**: Tools like **Slack**, **Microsoft Teams**, and **Zoom** enable real-time communication between team members. These tools are essential for remote teams to stay in sync and resolve issues quickly.
- **CI/CD Tools**: Jenkins, CircleCI, Travis CI, and GitLab CI/CD automate the integration and deployment process, ensuring that code is continuously tested and delivered.

Performance Optimization in Software Development

Performance optimization is a critical aspect of software development that focuses on improving the speed, responsiveness, and resource usage of a program. Optimizing performance involves writing efficient code, managing memory effectively, and using profiling and benchmarking tools to identify bottlenecks. Performance can be the difference between a smooth, fast user experience and an application that is slow, unresponsive, or resource-intensive.

Writing Efficient Code

The first step toward optimizing performance is writing efficient code. Efficient code is code that performs its tasks using minimal resources such as CPU, memory, and time. The key to efficient code is understanding the underlying algorithms and data structures, making conscious trade-offs, and avoiding common performance pitfalls. Here are several strategies for writing efficient code:

1. Choosing the Right Algorithm

One of the most important factors affecting the performance of software is the choice of algorithm. An inefficient algorithm can lead to significant performance degradation, especially as the input size grows. For example, an algorithm with a time complexity of $O(n^2)$ will be much slower than one with a time complexity of $O(n)$ as the size of the input increases.

Key considerations for choosing the right algorithm:

- **Time complexity**: Always try to choose algorithms with the best time complexity for the problem at hand. For example, quicksort ($O(n \log n)$) is generally faster than bubble sort ($O(n^2)$) for sorting large datasets.
- **Space complexity**: Consider the memory usage of the algorithm, especially for large datasets. Algorithms that require extra memory for data structures may not be optimal if memory usage is a concern.
- **Optimization strategies**: Use techniques such as **memoization, dynamic programming,** or **greedy algorithms** to optimize problem-solving.

2. Efficient Use of Data Structures

Selecting the right data structure is equally important for performance optimization. Using the appropriate data structure can lead to more efficient code in terms of both time and space complexity. For example, using a **hash table** for fast lookups instead of a list (which would require linear searching) can drastically improve performance.

Examples of choosing efficient data structures:

- **Arrays/Lists**: Useful when you need ordered collections of elements and frequent access by index. However, inserting or deleting elements at arbitrary positions can be slow.
- **Hash Tables (Dictionaries)**: Useful for fast lookups and insertions.
- **Queues and Stacks**: Efficient for processing elements in a specific order (first-in, first-out for queues, and last-in, first-out for stacks).
- **Trees (e.g., Binary Search Trees)**: Useful for maintaining ordered collections of data and performing fast insertions, deletions, and searches.
- **Graphs**: Used when modeling complex relationships between data points.

3. Avoiding Unnecessary Computations

Eliminate redundant operations in code. Repeated calculations or functions should be avoided, especially inside loops. Consider storing the results of expensive computations and reusing them when necessary. This practice can significantly reduce execution time.

Examples:

- **Memoization**: Storing results of expensive function calls and returning the cached result when the same inputs occur again.
- **Lazy evaluation**: Deferring computation until it is actually needed, rather than performing it upfront.

4. Optimizing Loops

Loops are often the most performance-critical part of an application. Efficient loop construction and minimizing unnecessary iterations can have a significant impact on performance.

Loop optimization techniques:

- **Loop unrolling**: This is a technique where multiple iterations of a loop are performed within a single iteration, reducing the overhead associated with the loop.
- **Avoid nested loops**: Nested loops often have exponential time complexity. Consider flattening or restructuring the loop to reduce overhead.

5. Minimizing I/O Operations

Input and output (I/O) operations, such as reading from files, writing to databases, or interacting with the network, are generally much slower than in-memory computations. Reducing the number of I/O operations and minimizing their complexity is crucial for performance optimization.

Tips for I/O optimization:

- **Batch operations**: Perform I/O in bulk to reduce the overhead of opening/closing files or making multiple network requests.

- **Asynchronous I/O**: Use asynchronous or non-blocking I/O operations when possible to avoid blocking the main thread of the application.

Memory Management

Memory management is another key aspect of performance optimization. Efficient memory usage can drastically improve the performance of an application, especially when dealing with large datasets or operating in resource-constrained environments.

1. Memory Allocation

Memory allocation refers to the process of allocating memory for variables and data structures during the execution of a program. Inefficient memory allocation can lead to performance problems such as excessive memory usage, fragmentation, and slowdowns due to frequent allocation/deallocation.

Memory management best practices:

- **Reuse memory**: Instead of repeatedly allocating and deallocating memory, try to reuse memory buffers or data structures.
- **Avoid memory leaks**: A memory leak occurs when a program fails to release memory that is no longer in use. Always ensure that memory is freed when it is no longer needed.

2. Garbage Collection (GC) and Manual Memory Management

In some programming languages (like Python, Java, and JavaScript), memory management is handled automatically via **garbage collection** (GC). While GC simplifies programming, it can introduce performance overhead, especially when garbage collectors run frequently.

To optimize garbage collection:

- **Minimize object creation**: Reusing existing objects rather than creating new ones can help reduce the load on the garbage collector.

- **Object pooling**: Reusing a pool of pre-allocated objects can help avoid the overhead of frequent allocations and deallocations.

In languages that do not have automatic garbage collection (such as C and C++), developers must manually allocate and free memory. In these cases, tools like **valgrind** or **AddressSanitizer** can be used to check for memory leaks and access violations.

3. Stack vs. Heap Memory

Understanding the difference between stack and heap memory is important for optimizing memory usage:

- **Stack**: Memory allocated on the stack is fast but limited. It is usually used for small, short-lived variables.
- **Heap**: Memory allocated on the heap is more flexible and used for dynamically

allocated objects or large data structures. However, heap allocation is slower and can lead to fragmentation if not managed carefully.

Optimize memory usage by allocating small, short-lived variables on the stack and larger, long-lived objects on the heap.

Profiling and Benchmarking

To effectively optimize performance, it is crucial to first understand where the bottlenecks are in your application. Profiling and benchmarking tools allow developers to measure performance and identify slow sections of code.

1. Profiling Tools

Profiling tools analyze the execution of your program to determine which functions, lines of code, or sections of the program consume the most time and resources. Profilers help identify performance bottlenecks, memory leaks, and inefficient code that can be optimized.

Common profiling tools:

- **gprof (GNU Profiler)**: A profiler for C/C++ programs that provides a detailed report on the time spent in each function.
- **Python's cProfile**: A profiler for Python that helps identify slow-running parts of the code.
- **Visual Studio Profiler**: A tool integrated with Visual Studio to profile and optimize C# and C++ applications.
- **Chrome DevTools**: Used to profile JavaScript code in web applications, measuring script performance and identifying slow functions.

2. Benchmarking Tools

Benchmarking involves testing the performance of code by running it under controlled conditions and measuring the execution time or resource usage. This allows developers to compare different approaches and measure the impact of optimizations.

Common benchmarking tools:

- **Benchmark.js**: A benchmarking library for JavaScript that helps developers measure the performance of code snippets.
- **JMH (Java Microbenchmarking Harness)**: A Java-based benchmarking tool for measuring performance of micro-level code snippets.
- **time**: A command-line utility on Unix-like systems for measuring the time taken by a command to execute.

3. Performance Tuning

Once you have identified bottlenecks through profiling and benchmarking, you can focus on optimizing the areas that will have the most significant impact. Common performance tuning techniques include:

- **Reducing algorithmic complexity**: Optimize the underlying algorithm to reduce time and space complexity.
- **Optimizing database queries**: Use indexing, batch operations, and caching to speed up database interactions.
- **Parallelization**: Use parallel computing or multi-threading to distribute tasks across multiple cores and improve performance for CPU-bound operations.

Summary

1. **Writing efficient code** involves using the right algorithms, data structures, avoiding redundant operations, and minimizing expensive I/O operations.
2. **Memory management** plays a significant role in performance optimization. Efficient use of memory, avoiding memory leaks, and understanding the difference between stack and heap allocation can help improve performance.

3. **Profiling and benchmarking** are essential for identifying bottlenecks and testing the impact of optimizations. Tools like gprof, cProfile, and Benchmark.js help analyze performance and guide optimization efforts.

Emerging Trends in Programming

The world of programming is constantly evolving, with new technologies and paradigms emerging that significantly impact how developers approach coding, designing, and deploying applications. The rise of **AI and machine learning**, **cloud computing and serverless applications**, and **Internet of Things (IoT) and embedded programming** represent some of the most exciting and transformative trends in the software development landscape. These trends are pushing the boundaries of what can be accomplished with code, enabling developers to create smarter, more efficient, and more connected systems.

AI and Machine Learning Programming

Artificial Intelligence (AI) and Machine Learning (ML) have become game-changers in the world of programming, enabling machines to learn from data and perform tasks that traditionally required human intelligence. AI and ML are transforming industries, including healthcare, finance, retail, and entertainment, and are becoming a major area of focus for developers.

1. What is AI and Machine Learning?

- **AI** refers to the simulation of human intelligence in machines that are programmed to think, reason, and learn. AI systems can perform tasks such as recognizing speech, translating languages, identifying images, and making decisions.

- **Machine Learning** is a subset of AI that allows systems to learn from data without

being explicitly programmed. ML
algorithms improve their performance
over time by analyzing patterns in large
datasets.

2. AI/ML Programming Paradigms

Programming for AI and ML involves different
paradigms and tools compared to traditional
software development:

- **Supervised Learning**: Involves training a
  model on labeled data, where the output is
  known. The model learns the relationship
  between input and output to make
  predictions on new, unseen data.

- **Unsupervised Learning**: Involves
  training models on unlabeled data,
  allowing the system to find patterns and
  groupings within the data on its own.
  Clustering and anomaly detection are
  common tasks in this paradigm.

- **Reinforcement Learning**: A type of ML where an agent learns to make decisions by interacting with an environment. It receives feedback in the form of rewards or penalties and aims to maximize cumulative rewards over time.

- **Deep Learning**: A subfield of ML focused on neural networks with many layers (hence "deep") that can model complex relationships and patterns in data. Deep learning is used in tasks like image recognition, natural language processing (NLP), and autonomous driving.

3. Tools and Libraries for AI/ML Development

To develop AI and ML applications, programmers use a variety of frameworks and libraries that simplify the implementation of complex algorithms:

- **TensorFlow**: An open-source library developed by Google, widely used for building and training deep learning models.
- **PyTorch**: A dynamic machine learning framework developed by Facebook, known for its ease of use and flexibility in building deep learning models.
- **scikit-learn**: A Python library for machine learning that provides simple and efficient tools for data mining and data analysis.
- **Keras**: An open-source deep learning framework built on top of TensorFlow that allows for easy and quick prototyping of neural networks.
- **OpenCV**: A computer vision library used for real-time image and video processing.

4. Challenges in AI/ML Programming

Developing AI and ML applications presents several challenges:

- **Data quality and quantity**: High-quality labeled data is critical for training AI and ML models. Obtaining large datasets for training can be time-consuming and expensive.
- **Model interpretability**: Deep learning models, especially neural networks, are often seen as "black boxes." Understanding how models make decisions and ensuring they are explainable is an ongoing challenge.
- **Computational resources**: Training AI and ML models, particularly deep learning models, requires significant computational power. Developers often rely on GPUs and cloud computing to train large models efficiently.

5. Future of AI and Machine Learning Programming

The future of AI and machine learning will likely focus on **AI ethics**, **edge computing**, and **autonomous systems**. As AI becomes more integrated into everyday applications, ethical considerations around privacy, bias, and accountability will play a crucial role in its development.

Cloud Computing and Serverless Applications

Cloud computing has revolutionized how software is developed, deployed, and maintained, offering scalability, flexibility, and cost-efficiency. Serverless computing, a newer paradigm within cloud computing, abstracts the infrastructure layer and allows developers to focus solely on writing code without worrying about managing servers.

1. What is Cloud Computing?

Cloud computing is the delivery of computing services (including storage, processing, and networking) over the internet ("the cloud"). Rather than relying on on-premise hardware, cloud services allow organizations and developers to access computing resources on-demand, paying only for what they use.

2. Key Benefits of Cloud Computing

- **Scalability**: Cloud platforms enable automatic scaling, allowing applications to handle varying loads without manual intervention.
- **Cost-efficiency**: Developers only pay for the resources they use, which reduces upfront infrastructure costs.
- **Availability**: Cloud services typically offer high availability and fault tolerance, ensuring that applications remain accessible and operational.
- **Flexibility**: Cloud platforms support a wide variety of services, including compute instances, storage, databases, and machine learning, all of which can be accessed remotely.

3. Serverless Computing: A New Paradigm

Serverless computing allows developers to build and deploy applications without managing the underlying infrastructure. Rather than provisioning and managing servers, developers write functions that are triggered by events, and the cloud provider automatically handles the execution of those functions.

- **Function-as-a-Service (FaaS)**: Serverless applications are built around small units of code called functions, which are triggered by specific events (such as HTTP requests, file uploads, or database updates).
- **Event-driven architecture**: Serverless applications are typically event-driven, meaning they respond to external events in real-time.
- **Auto-scaling**: Serverless platforms automatically scale resources based on the workload, without the developer needing to manage scaling.

4. Popular Cloud and Serverless Platforms

- **AWS Lambda**: A serverless computing service provided by Amazon Web Services (AWS) that allows developers to run code in response to events without managing servers.
- **Google Cloud Functions**: A serverless compute service by Google that lets developers run event-driven functions in the cloud.
- **Azure Functions**: A serverless compute service by Microsoft Azure that enables developers to execute code in response to events.

5. Challenges and Considerations

- **Cold starts**: When a serverless function is triggered after being idle for a while, there may be a slight delay in its execution. This is called a "cold start."
- **Vendor lock-in**: Since serverless applications are tied to specific cloud providers, switching between providers can be difficult and costly.

- **Monitoring and debugging**: The distributed nature of serverless applications can make it harder to track down issues and monitor performance.

6. The Future of Cloud and Serverless Computing

Serverless computing is likely to become more advanced, with increased support for complex, long-running tasks and integration with AI and machine learning services. Furthermore, **hybrid cloud** and **multi-cloud** environments will enable developers to create flexible and cost-effective infrastructure solutions.

Internet of Things (IoT) and Embedded Programming

The **Internet of Things (IoT)** refers to the network of physical devices, vehicles, and appliances embedded with sensors, software, and other technologies to connect and exchange data with other devices and systems over the internet.

As IoT applications proliferate, embedded programming becomes a key component of developing connected devices that are intelligent, responsive, and resource-efficient.

1. What is IoT and Embedded Programming?

- **IoT** refers to the interconnection of everyday physical objects that communicate with each other and with centralized systems over the internet. These devices include everything from smart thermostats and refrigerators to industrial sensors and healthcare monitors.
- **Embedded programming** involves writing software for embedded systems—small, specialized computing devices often with limited resources (CPU, memory, power). These systems are designed to perform specific functions and are often integrated into hardware.

2. IoT Applications

IoT has wide-ranging applications across various industries:

- **Smart homes**: Devices like smart thermostats, lighting systems, and voice assistants that automate and optimize home functions.
- **Healthcare**: IoT-enabled devices such as wearables, remote monitoring devices, and smart implants that improve patient care and health monitoring.
- **Agriculture**: Sensors for monitoring soil moisture, weather conditions, and crop health to optimize farming practices.
- **Industry**: IoT devices are used in manufacturing for predictive maintenance, real-time monitoring, and automation.

3. Challenges in IoT and Embedded Programming

- **Power efficiency**: Many IoT devices are battery-powered, making power consumption a critical consideration.

Efficient code and hardware are required to extend battery life.

- **Security**: IoT devices often collect sensitive data and can be vulnerable to hacking. Implementing secure communication, encryption, and authentication is crucial for protecting devices and data.
- **Connectivity**: IoT devices need reliable and low-latency connectivity to function effectively, often relying on Wi-Fi, Bluetooth, Zigbee, or 5G networks.

4. Tools for IoT and Embedded Development

- **Arduino**: An open-source electronics platform that provides microcontroller-based boards for developing embedded applications.
- **Raspberry Pi**: A small, affordable computer used for building DIY embedded systems and IoT applications.
- **ESP32/ESP8266**: Wi-Fi-enabled microcontrollers used for building connected IoT devices.

- **Embedded C/C++**: Languages commonly used for

programming embedded systems due to their ability to efficiently control hardware resources.

5. Future of IoT and Embedded Programming

The future of IoT and embedded systems will be heavily influenced by advancements in 5G networks, edge computing, and AI. **Edge computing** will allow IoT devices to process data locally rather than relying on cloud servers, improving performance and reducing latency. Additionally, as IoT becomes more pervasive, **interoperability** between devices from different manufacturers will become a major focus, along with **AI-driven automation** for intelligent decision-making.

Building a Programming Portfolio

A programming portfolio is an essential tool for developers, showcasing their skills, accomplishments, and personal projects. In today's competitive job market, having a strong portfolio can make a significant difference when applying for jobs or freelance opportunities. A well-crafted portfolio highlights a developer's technical proficiency, problem-solving abilities, and creativity, offering employers and clients a tangible representation of their work.

1. Creating Personal Projects

Personal projects are the cornerstone of a programming portfolio. They demonstrate your ability to apply programming skills to real-world problems, exhibit your creativity, and show your dedication to continuous learning. Well-executed projects are often what set you apart from other candidates.

1.1. Identifying Project Ideas

When building personal projects, it's essential to choose ideas that reflect both your interests and skills. Here are some tips for selecting the right project ideas:

- **Solve a real-world problem**: Identify issues you face in your everyday life or challenges in industries you are passionate about. Developing a project to solve a problem can be motivating and showcase your ability to think critically.

- **Showcase your strengths**: Select projects that highlight your strongest technical skills or areas of expertise. For instance, if you excel in machine learning, build a recommendation system. If web development is your focus, create an interactive, user-friendly website or app.

- **Keep it manageable**: Start with smaller projects that are feasible given your skill level, but make sure they are complex enough to demonstrate your abilities. Gradually increase the complexity of your projects as you grow in confidence and skill.

- **Explore trending technologies**: Stay up to date with the latest trends in programming and technology, such as **AI**, **blockchain**, **cloud computing**, **mobile development**, or **web development frameworks**. Projects that incorporate cutting-edge technologies can attract attention from potential employers.

1.2. Types of Personal Projects

Here are some types of personal projects that can be added to a programming portfolio:

- **Web applications**: Build websites or web apps that demonstrate your front-end and back-end development skills. You could create an e-commerce site, a blog platform, or a task manager.

- **Mobile apps**: Develop apps for Android or iOS to showcase your mobile development capabilities. Projects like a weather app, chat application, or fitness tracker can demonstrate different skills.

- **Machine learning models**: If you are working with AI, create a project that uses machine learning to solve a real-world problem, such as a classifier, recommendation engine, or a natural language processing (NLP) application.

- **Automation tools**: Automate mundane tasks with scripts or tools, like web scraping bots, data analysis pipelines, or file management systems.

- **Games**: If you are passionate about game development, consider creating a simple 2D or 3D game using engines like **Unity** or **Godot**. Games demonstrate a wide range of skills, including logic, algorithms, and user experience design.

- **Open-source contributions**: Contributing to open-source projects shows that you can work collaboratively and contribute to the broader programming community. It also demonstrates your ability to navigate large codebases and collaborate with others.

1.3. Building a Portfolio of Projects

When you build personal projects, make sure to:

- **Ensure quality and polish**: A project in your portfolio should be clean, functional, and well-documented. Test it thoroughly, address bugs, and ensure a positive user experience.
- **Focus on scalability**: While it's okay to start small, ensure that your projects are designed with scalability in mind. This demonstrates that you can think ahead and create maintainable, extensible code.

1.4. Code Repositories and Version Control

For each personal project, use version control systems like **Git** to track changes and collaborate with others. Host your code on platforms like **GitHub**, **GitLab**, or **Bitbucket**. Having a well-organized, version-controlled code repository provides potential employers with insight into your coding habits and demonstrates your proficiency with industry-standard tools.

2. Documenting Your Work

Documentation is essential to a programming portfolio as it helps others understand your projects and how to use them. It also highlights your ability to communicate technical information clearly—a key skill for developers.

2.1. Writing Clear ReadMe Files

A well-written **README** file is the first thing visitors will encounter when viewing your project repository. It should contain essential information such as:

- **Project description**: Explain what the project does, its purpose, and the problem it solves.
- **Technologies used**: List the programming languages, frameworks, libraries, and tools you used to build the project.
- **Setup instructions**: Provide clear, step-by-step instructions on how to set up the project locally. Include dependencies,

environment variables, and installation steps.

- **Usage guide**: Describe how to run the project, any commands that need to be executed, and how to use the application.
- **Contributing**: If you're open to contributions, provide guidelines on how others can contribute to the project.
- **Screenshots or demo links**: Include visual aids like screenshots, GIFs, or a live demo of your project to help potential employers or collaborators understand what it looks like and how it works.

2.2. Writing Comments and Documentation in Code

- **Inline comments**: Use comments to explain why you have implemented specific parts of your code in a certain way, especially for complex algorithms or logic.
- **Function and module documentation**: Document the purpose and parameters of functions, methods, and classes with clear

docstrings or comments. This improves the readability and maintainability of your code.

2.3. Portfolio Website

Consider creating a **personal portfolio website** to showcase your projects, skills, and experiences in a more interactive and visually appealing format. Include:

- A brief introduction about yourself, your background, and your career goals.
- A showcase of your best projects with links to their code repositories and live demos.
- A contact form or email address for potential employers to reach out.

Use **responsive design** to ensure your portfolio works on both desktop and mobile devices. Make the user experience smooth and intuitive, as this will also reflect your attention to detail in coding.

3. Preparing for Interviews and Job Applications

A programming portfolio is an invaluable asset when applying for jobs, but it's not enough to simply create a portfolio and wait for offers. The next step is preparing for interviews and making sure your application stands out to hiring managers.

3.1. Tailoring Your Portfolio for Specific Roles

When applying for a job, tailor your portfolio to the specific position you're seeking. For example:

- **Web developer**: Emphasize web development projects, front-end frameworks (like React or Angular), and back-end technologies (like Node.js or Django).
- **Machine learning engineer**: Highlight ML-related projects, such as neural

networks, natural language processing, or data visualization.

- **Mobile developer**: Focus on mobile apps you've built, showcasing your skills with Android (Java/Kotlin) or iOS (Swift) development.

3.2. Preparing for Technical Interviews

Technical interviews often involve solving coding problems on the spot. To prepare for coding challenges:

- **Practice problem-solving**: Use platforms like **LeetCode**, **HackerRank**, or **CodeSignal** to practice solving algorithmic problems and data structure questions.
- **Brush up on data structures and algorithms**: Review the fundamentals of algorithms, sorting, searching, and common data structures like linked lists, trees, stacks, and queues.
- **Write clean, efficient code**: Focus on writing readable, well-documented code

that demonstrates your understanding of optimization and problem-solving strategies.

- **Explain your thought process**: During the interview, clearly explain how you approach the problem and the trade-offs you're making in your solution.

3.3. Mock Interviews

Participate in mock interviews with peers or mentors to simulate the real interview experience. Websites like **Pramp** and **Interviewing.io** offer free mock technical interviews with industry professionals.

3.4. Preparing for Behavioral Interviews

Behavioral interviews assess how well you work in a team, handle challenges, and approach problem-solving in a professional context. Prepare for behavioral interviews by:

- Reviewing common questions like "Tell me about a time you faced a challenge" or "How do you handle tight deadlines?"

- Using the **STAR method** (Situation, Task, Action, Result) to structure your answers and provide clear, concise responses.

3.5. Building Your Online Presence

Having a strong online presence can make you more visible to potential employers:

- **LinkedIn**: Keep your LinkedIn profile up to date with your projects, skills, and experiences. Link to your portfolio website and GitHub repositories.
- **GitHub**: Keep your GitHub active and organized, contributing to projects and showing your involvement in the coding community.
- **Networking**: Attend programming meetups, conferences, and webinars to network with others in the industry and stay up to date with the latest trends.

Resources for Continued Learning

The field of programming is vast and constantly evolving. As a developer, it's essential to keep learning new languages, tools, techniques, and best practices to stay competitive and relevant in the industry. Fortunately, there is an abundance of resources available to support your learning journey. These resources range from books and tutorials to online courses, open-source contributions, and active communities where you can network with other developers.

---

1. Books, Tutorials, and Online Courses

1.1. Books

Books are a great way to get deep insights into programming concepts, best practices, and language-specific techniques. Many developers consider books to be an essential part of their learning toolkit, especially for mastering fundamental concepts that can apply across multiple programming languages.

Recommended Books for Developers:

- **"Clean Code: A Handbook of Agile Software Craftsmanship" by Robert C. Martin**
  A classic book that teaches you how to write clean, readable, and maintainable code. It emphasizes principles such as proper naming, refactoring, and code organization.

- **"The Pragmatic Programmer: Your Journey to Mastery" by Andrew Hunt and David Thomas**
  A well-regarded book offering advice on

software development techniques and best practices. It touches on debugging, testing, and building flexible, reusable code.

- **"You Don't Know JS" by Kyle Simpson**
 This book series is a deep dive into JavaScript, covering the language's core concepts and nuances. It is ideal for developers who want to gain a comprehensive understanding of JavaScript.

- **"Design Patterns: Elements of Reusable Object-Oriented Software" by Erich Gamma, Richard Helm, Ralph Johnson, and John Vlissides**
 A foundational book for learning design patterns, which are proven solutions to common software design problems. It is essential for understanding how to build scalable, maintainable, and flexible software systems.

- **"Python Crash Course" by Eric Matthes**
  A hands-on introduction to Python programming, ideal for beginners. It covers the basics and guides readers through projects, such as building games and web applications.

- **"Algorithms" by Robert Sedgewick and Kevin Wayne**
  A well-structured book that provides an introduction to algorithms and data structures. It offers a mix of theory and practical exercises to help you understand and apply algorithms in real-world scenarios.

1.2. Tutorials

Online tutorials offer interactive, step-by-step guidance on how to learn programming, solve specific problems, or build projects. Tutorials are often designed to be hands-on, making them ideal for learning by doing.

Popular Tutorial Platforms:

- **Codecademy**
  Codecademy offers interactive coding lessons in a variety of languages, including Python, JavaScript, Ruby, and more. The platform offers beginner-friendly tutorials as well as intermediate and advanced content.

- **freeCodeCamp**
  freeCodeCamp provides free coding lessons in web development, data structures, algorithms, and more. It features hands-on projects and certifications to help learners build real-world skills.

- **Khan Academy**
  Known for its accessible approach to teaching various subjects, Khan Academy offers programming tutorials on topics like JavaScript, HTML/CSS, and SQL,

with a focus on interactive learning.

- **Udemy**
  Udemy has a wide range of video-based programming tutorials taught by industry professionals. Courses span beginner to advanced topics and cover everything from basic syntax to advanced algorithms.

- **W3Schools**
  A great resource for beginners, W3Schools provides tutorials on web development technologies like HTML, CSS, JavaScript, and SQL. Each tutorial is accompanied by examples and exercises to reinforce learning.

- **The Odin Project**
  The Odin Project offers a comprehensive, free curriculum focused on full-stack web development. It provides in-depth tutorials and projects to help learners build practical programming skills.

1.3. Online Courses

Online courses, often offered by universities or independent platforms, provide structured learning paths and certifications. Many of these courses are taught by experts and feature assignments, quizzes, and peer interactions to help you learn effectively.

Top Platforms for Online Courses:

- **Coursera**

  Coursera offers high-quality courses from top universities and companies. You can take courses in computer science, web development, machine learning, and other advanced topics. Many courses are free to audit, with a fee for certificates.

- **edX**

  edX is another popular platform offering university-style courses on a wide range of topics, including software development, data science, and algorithms. Some courses are free, while others require a paid certificate.

- **Udacity**
  Udacity is known for its "Nanodegree" programs, which are specialized, industry-focused courses that dive deep into specific areas like data science, machine learning, and web development. These are great for those who want to focus on a particular career path.

- **Pluralsight**
  Pluralsight is an online platform offering courses for developers, IT professionals, and creative artists. It has a wide selection of content covering programming languages, frameworks, and specific technologies like cloud computing and security.

---

2. Open-Source Contributions

Contributing to open-source projects is an excellent way to learn, improve your skills, and build a network of professional contacts. It offers you the opportunity to work on real-world projects, collaborate with other developers, and understand large codebases.

2.1. How to Start Contributing to Open Source

- **Find Projects That Interest You**: Search for open-source repositories on GitHub, GitLab, or Bitbucket that align with your skills and interests. Look for projects labeled with "good first issue" for beginner-friendly tasks.

- **Understand the Contribution Process**: Familiarize yourself with the contributing guidelines of the repository. Most projects have clear instructions on how to fork the repository, make changes, and submit pull requests.

- **Start Small**: Begin by fixing bugs, improving documentation, or adding small features. This will help you get comfortable with the contribution process without feeling overwhelmed.

- **Collaborate and Ask for Help**: Open-source communities are often very welcoming. Don't be afraid to ask questions or seek help from other contributors.

- **Keep Learning**: Working on open-source projects exposes you to different coding styles and problem-solving approaches, allowing you to learn from others and expand your skill set.

2.2. Popular Open-Source Platforms

- **GitHub**
  GitHub is the largest open-source platform and offers a plethora of repositories on a wide range of topics. It's

a great place to find projects to contribute to and learn from.

- **GitLab**
  Similar to GitHub, GitLab offers open-source projects and tools for version control and collaboration. It also provides features for continuous integration and deployment (CI/CD).

- **SourceForge**
  SourceForge is one of the oldest open-source platforms and hosts many legacy projects. While GitHub and GitLab have taken the lead in popularity, SourceForge still maintains a large number of projects.

---

3. Communities and Networking

Being part of a programming community helps you stay motivated, learn from others, and discover new opportunities. Online communities, conferences, and meetups provide avenues to connect with fellow developers, share knowledge, and get feedback on your projects.

3.1. Online Communities

- **Stack Overflow**
  Stack Overflow is one of the most popular programming Q&A sites, where you can ask technical questions, share solutions, and engage with other developers. It's a fantastic resource for troubleshooting specific problems and learning from community answers.

- **Reddit**
  Subreddits like **r/learnprogramming**, **r/coding**, and **r/programming** are great places to engage with other developers, share your knowledge, or seek advice on coding-related topics.

- **Dev.to**
  Dev.to is a social platform for developers

where you can share articles, tutorials, and experiences. It's a friendly, inclusive community of developers who help each other learn and grow.

- **Slack and Discord Communities**
  Many programming communities now use **Slack** or **Discord** for real-time chat and collaboration. Join channels dedicated to specific programming languages or frameworks to engage with others in the field.

- **GitHub Discussions**
  GitHub Discussions allows developers to ask questions, share ideas, and participate in open-source projects. It's a great way to connect with other contributors to projects you're involved with.

3.2. Networking and Career Development

- **LinkedIn**
  LinkedIn is an essential tool for

networking, job searching, and staying up to date with industry trends. Join relevant groups, share your achievements, and engage with industry experts to expand your network.

- **Meetups and Conferences**
  Attending **meetups**, **hackathons**, and **conferences** (both virtual and in-person) provides opportunities to connect with professionals, learn from industry leaders, and stay informed about the latest trends in programming.

- **Mentorship**
  Seek out mentors who can offer guidance and help you navigate your career. Mentorship programs, both formal and informal, can be found through organizations, coding bootcamps, or networking platforms.

Glossary of Terms in Programming

A

- **Algorithm**: A step-by-step procedure or formula for solving a problem or performing a task.
- **API (Application Programming Interface)**: A set of protocols and tools for building software and applications, allowing different programs to communicate with each other.
- **Array**: A data structure that stores a collection of elements, typically of the

same data type, at contiguous memory locations.

- **Asynchronous**: A programming technique that allows tasks to run independently of the main program flow, often used for handling I/O operations without blocking the execution of other code.

- **Automation**: The use of technology to perform tasks without human intervention, often implemented in programming to streamline repetitive or complex processes.

- **Abstraction**: A principle in programming that involves hiding complex implementation details and showing only the essential features of an object or system.

B

- **Backend**: The server-side part of a web application or software that handles the business logic, database interaction, and data processing, often interacting with the front end.

- **Boolean**: A data type that can only have two values: true or false. It is often used in conditional statements and logic operations.
- **Bug**: An error or flaw in a program that causes it to behave unexpectedly or incorrectly.
- **Branch**: A version of a repository in version control, typically used to develop features, fix bugs, or experiment in isolation from the main codebase.

C

- **Class**: A blueprint for creating objects in object-oriented programming (OOP). It defines the properties and behaviors that the objects created from it will have.
- **CLI (Command-Line Interface)**: A text-based interface used to interact with a computer program by typing commands instead of using a graphical interface.

- **Compiler**: A program that translates source code written in a high-level programming language into machine code or intermediate code.
- **Commit**: In version control systems like Git, a commit is a snapshot of the changes made to a repository.
- **Conditional Statement**: A statement that allows for decision-making in code, often using if, else, or switch to execute different blocks of code based on specific conditions.
- **Constructor**: A special function in object-oriented programming that is called when an object is created, initializing its properties.

D

- **Data Structure**: A way of organizing and storing data in a computer so that it can be accessed and manipulated efficiently.
- **Database**: A structured collection of data stored in a way that allows for easy retrieval, insertion, and modification.

Databases can be relational (SQL) or non-relational (NoSQL).

- **Debugger**: A tool used to test and debug programs by allowing developers to step through the code, inspect variables, and identify errors.
- **Deploy**: The process of moving software or an application from development to a production environment, making it available for users.
- **Data Type**: A classification that specifies which type of value a variable can hold, such as integers, floating-point numbers, or strings.
- **Docker**: A platform for developing, shipping, and running applications inside lightweight, portable containers.

E

- **Exception**: An event that disrupts the normal flow of program execution, typically caused by errors like invalid input or file not found.

- **Encapsulation**: A principle of object-oriented programming that involves bundling data and the methods that operate on that data into a single unit or class.
- **Expression**: A combination of variables, constants, operators, and functions that produce a value when evaluated.
- **Event-Driven Programming**: A programming paradigm where the flow of the program is determined by events such as user actions or sensor outputs, common in GUI development and asynchronous programming.
- **Ecosystem**: The combination of tools, frameworks, libraries, and other software that support the development of applications within a particular environment, such as the JavaScript or Python ecosystem.

F

- **Framework**: A set of pre-written code or libraries designed to simplify and standardize the development of applications, often providing templates and structures.

- **Function**: A block of code that performs a specific task and can be called to execute with inputs (parameters) and return outputs (values).
- **Fork**: A copy of a repository in version control systems like Git, allowing a developer to freely experiment with changes without affecting the original project.
- **Front-End**: The client-side part of a web application, responsible for user interactions and user interface (UI) design.
- **Framework**: A pre-built set of tools and libraries for developers that makes it easier to build applications.

G

- **Git**: A distributed version control system used to track changes in code during development, allowing multiple developers to collaborate on a project.

- **GitHub**: A web-based platform for hosting Git repositories and facilitating collaboration on software projects.
- **Garbage Collection**: The automatic process of reclaiming memory that is no longer in use by the program, typically implemented in languages like Java and Python.
- **GUI (Graphical User Interface)**: A visual interface that allows users to interact with software using graphical icons, buttons, and menus, as opposed to a command-line interface.

H

- **Hash Table**: A data structure that stores key-value pairs, where keys are hashed into a unique index to allow for fast lookups.
- **HTML (HyperText Markup Language)**: The standard markup language used to create and structure content on the web.
- **HTTP (Hypertext Transfer Protocol)**: A protocol used for transferring web pages

and data across the internet between clients and servers.

- **Hacker**: A person who is skilled in computer programming and system design, often associated with creative problem-solving and exploration of technology.

I

- **IDE (Integrated Development Environment)**: A software application that provides comprehensive tools for writing, testing, and debugging code, such as code editors, compilers, and debuggers.
- **Inheritance**: An object-oriented programming feature that allows a class to inherit properties and methods from another class.
- **Interface**: A contract or blueprint that defines a set of methods or properties that a class must implement, but does not provide the actual implementation.
- **Instance**: A specific realization of a class in object-oriented programming. An

object created from a class is an instance of that class.
- **Index**: A numerical representation of an element's position within a collection, such as an array or list.

J

- **JavaScript**: A high-level, interpreted programming language primarily used for creating interactive elements on web pages.
- **JVM (Java Virtual Machine)**: A virtual machine that enables Java programs to run on any device or platform without modification.
- **JQuery**: A fast, small, and feature-rich JavaScript library designed to simplify tasks such as DOM manipulation, event handling, and AJAX calls.

K

- **Kernel**: The core part of an operating system that manages system resources, hardware, and communication between software and hardware components.

- **Kubernetes**: An open-source platform for automating the deployment, scaling, and management of containerized applications.

L

- **Library**: A collection of pre-written code that developers can use to perform common tasks, such as handling HTTP requests or parsing JSON data.
- **Lambda Function**: A small anonymous function in programming that is typically used for short-lived operations, often passed as arguments to other functions.
- **Loop**: A programming construct used to repeat a set of instructions a specific number of times or while a condition is true, e.g., for, while, and do-while loops.

M

- **Middleware**: Software that provides services and communication between different applications, often used in web applications to handle requests, authentication, and error handling.
- **MVC (Model-View-Controller)**: A design pattern for developing user interfaces that separates data (model), user interface (view), and the logic (controller).
- **Machine Learning**: A subset of artificial intelligence (AI) where algorithms improve automatically through experience and data.

N

- **Node**: A basic unit of data in a structure, such as a linked list or tree, or a term used in server environments (e.g., Node.js) to refer to the server-side JavaScript runtime environment.
- **Null**: A special value in programming representing the absence of a value or object.

- **NoSQL**: A type of database that does not use the traditional relational model, often used for large-scale, distributed data storage with flexible schema.

O

- **Object-Oriented Programming (OOP)**: A programming paradigm based on the concept of "objects," which bundle data and methods that operate on the data together.
- **Overloading**: The ability to define multiple methods or functions with the same name but different parameters in object-oriented programming.

P

- **Polymorphism**: An object-oriented programming concept that allows methods to take many forms, typically through inheritance or interfaces.
- **Prototype**: An early or preliminary version of a program or product, often

used for testing and development
purposes.
- **Python**: A high-level, interpreted
  programming language known for its
  simplicity and versatility, used in a wide
  range of fields, from web development to
  data science.

Q

- **Queue**: A linear data structure where
  elements are added at the rear and
  removed from the front, following the
  "first-in, first-out" (FIFO) principle.

R

- **Recursion**: A programming

technique where a function calls itself to solve a
problem, often used in tasks like sorting, tree
traversal, and solving mathematical problems.

- **REST (Representational State
  Transfer)**: An architectural style for

designing networked applications, often used in web services and APIs.

- **Ruby**: A high-level, interpreted programming language known for its simplicity and use in web development, particularly with the Ruby on Rails framework.

S

- **SQL (Structured Query Language)**: A language used to interact with relational databases, performing operations like querying, inserting, updating, and deleting data.
- **SaaS (Software as a Service)**: A cloud computing model where software is hosted and delivered over the internet, often via subscription.
- **Server**: A computer or program that provides services, resources, or data to other computers (clients) over a network.
- **Singleton**: A design pattern that restricts a class to have only one instance and provides a global point of access to it.

T

- **Token**: A unit of code or data, often referring to elements like keywords, operators, or symbols in programming languages.
- **Testing**: The process of running code through various scenarios to ensure it functions correctly and meets requirements, including unit tests, integration tests, and end-to-end tests.

U

- **Unit Test**: A type of test that checks the functionality of a specific part (unit) of the program, usually a function or method, in isolation.
- **UML (Unified Modeling Language)**: A standardized modeling language used to visualize the design of a software system, often through diagrams like class diagrams and sequence diagrams.

V

- **Version Control**: A system that records changes to files, allowing multiple developers to work on a project collaboratively without overwriting each other's work.
- **Virtual Machine**: A software emulation of a physical computer that runs its own operating system and applications, isolated from the host system.

W

- **Web API**: A type of API that allows different software applications to communicate over the web using protocols like HTTP.
- **WebSocket**: A protocol for enabling real-time, bidirectional communication between a client and server over a single, long-lived connection.

X

- **XML (eXtensible Markup Language)**: A markup language used to define rules for encoding documents in a format that is both human-readable and machine-readable.

Y

- **YAML (YAML Ain't Markup Language)**: A human-readable data serialization format often used for configuration files and data exchange between languages with different data structures.

Z

- **Zero-Day**: A term used to describe a previously unknown vulnerability in software that has not yet been patched or addressed by the vendor.
- **Zombie Process**: A process that has completed execution but still has an entry in the process table because it has not been properly cleaned up by the parent process.

Computer Programming Essentials

Computer Programming Essentials

Computer Programming Essentials